Adoption and Loss

The Hidden Grief

BY

EVELYN BURNS ROBINSON

First published in Australia in 2000 by

Clova Publications
PO Box 328
Christies Beach
South Australia.

ISBN 1 74053 000 4

In association with Jacobyte Books, Adelaide, South Australia, www.jacobytebooks.com

The author, Evelyn Robinson (née Burns), MA, Dip Ed, BSW, was born and raised in Renfrew, Scotland. She later emigrated to Bermuda and finally to Adelaide, South Australia, where she currently lives. She is a former high school teacher and the mother of five children, of whom she has raised four. She is currently a social worker employed by the Association Representing Mothers Separated from their children by adoption (ARMS). The author has presented the following conference and seminar papers:

Understanding the Loss of a Relinquishing Mother (co-presenter), *Understanding Loss and Managing Change*, National Multidisciplinary Conference, March, 1995, Adelaide, Australia.

Unmasking the Grief of Relinquishing Mothers, (co-presenter), *Unmasking Grief,* National Association for Loss and Grief, 9th Biennial National Conference, September, 1995, Adelaide, Australia.

What Does Reconciliation Mean for Natural Mothers, (co-presenter), *Sixth Australian Conference on Adoption,* June, 1997, Brisbane, Australia.

Grief Associated with the Loss of Children to Adoption, *Sixth Australian Conference on Adoption*, June, 1997, Brisbane, Australia.

Post-Relinquishment Grief Counselling, *2nd International Conference on Social Work in Health and Mental Health*, January, 1998, Melbourne, Australia.

Disenfranchised grief: recognising and meeting the needs of birth parents who have lost children to adoption, *British Association of Social Workers' Seminar*, Edinburgh, Scotland, August, 1998.

It is the author's intention to write a second book about adoption and for the purposes of that book, the author would welcome input from readers of this book. If you would like your experiences or comments to be considered for inclusion in that book, please forward them to the author by mail to the following address:

Clova Publications
PO Box 328
Christies Beach
South Australia 5165

or by e-mail to "clova49@hotmail.com".

Please indicate whether or not you would like your comments to be published anonymously.

Evelyn Robinson has written a book which will hold the reader's interest, whether a part of the adoption triangle or not. The first part of the book, which portrays her personal life's experiences, reads like a novel. Her own difficult childhood and the ensuing drama of her pregnancy and surrendering of her child finds a resonance in our hearts. In the second part, Ms Robinson sensitively and compassionately explains the tremendous loss experienced by all affected by adoption and suggests ways of dealing with this loss. She also gives an accurate accounting of the manner in which each part of the triangle experiences and responds to adoption reunion. Part 3 contains her own personal and political views of adoption.

I highly recommend this book as a wonderful addition to adoption literature, and fervently hope that it will be available in the United States.

Nancy Verrier, author
The Primal Wound: Understanding the adopted Child

****

(Ms Robinson's book)…is an honest and detailed account of one birth mother's experience of the pain and indignity of losing her son to adoption.

Ariel Bruce, social worker

****

(Ms Robinson's book) …is a valuable piece of work…a brave act that helps others know that they are not alone. Its value lies in … the hope that the book offers to others. There can never be enough birth mother stories like this.

Gary Clapton, Birthlink

This book is dedicated to my dear Mother, who showed more generosity of spirit in her life than anyone I ever knew.

CONTENTS

Introduction

PART 1: *Mistreated, mateless mother*

PART 2: *The grief caused by adoption loss*

PART 3: *What does it all mean?*

Introduction

I should like to make my position clear from the outset. I am the natural mother of an adult, adopted child. I am also a social worker, but one who would never work in the area of adoption placement. I approach the subject of adoption from a professional stance but I also approach it with a personal passion, for which I make no apology. I have written this book for all those whose lives have been affected by adoption, but especially for women who have lost children through adoption. I have written also for those who come in contact with them, whether socially or professionally. I know that many people will recognise themselves in the pages of this book. For those who read this book, I hope that it will make them laugh, I hope that it will make them cry, but most of all, I hope that it will make them think. For some people it will make them think of issues that they have never considered, for others I hope that it will encourage them to consider familiar issues in a new light. I believe that this book makes a valuable and positive contribution to the adoption debate. Some people inspire others and help them to heal by way of drama, art or music. I hope that I have done so by writing this book.

This book came to be written because, as part of my social work degree, I wrote a 6000 word essay entitled "Grief Associated with the Loss of Children to Adoption". The most interesting fact which emerged from my research for the essay was that women who had lost children through adoption reported that, not only did time not heal their pain at the loss of their children, but that, for most, their anger and sense of loss actually *increased* with the passage of time. This flew in the face of everything that I was learning about grief resolution. I went on to explore the nature of adoption-related grief and the particular factors which were operating to block the resolution of grief. After I graduated, I then presented a paper based on this essay at the Sixth Australian Adoption Conference in Brisbane in June 1997. After my presentation, I was approached by one of the workshop presenters at the conference, a Scottish woman called Liz, who said that she was very moved by my paper and asked, "Where can I buy your book?". I confessed to her that I had never written a book. She told me that she thought that I should. I received further encouragement from others who had heard my presentation and later from many who read my paper.

Throughout my research, I have found much of the work written *about* mothers who have lost children through adoption to be narrow-minded, patronising and sometimes downright infuriating. There are very few books written about the experience *by* the mothers themselves. For this reason I hope that my book will be welcomed, not only by natural mothers, but also by others affected by adoption and by those who have a genuine desire to understand. Anyone can express an opinion on adoption, but if they have no experience, either personal or professional, in the area, then their opinion may be of very limited value. I hope that, after reading my book, women who have not yet broken their silence about their lost children will have the courage to do so and that adopted people who have not yet searched for their original families will also have the courage to do so. Mothers who do not acknowledge their lost children and adopted people who do not acknowledge their original mothers are not living *authentically* because they are denying the existence of a person who is, in fact, whether physically present or not, an important contributor to their life's experience. I hope that I have shown that for natural parents and for adopted people, it is not forgetting your past and your history that allows you to go on with your life. Rather, it is acknowledging the past and honouring its impact that gives the present its meaning and bestows confidence for the future. It is my hope that this book will result in further revelations from those whose lives have been affected by adoption in order that the community might be educated and made aware of their issues.

My principal aim in writing this book is to increase awareness and understanding of the loss experienced by the natural mothers of adopted children and their resultant grief. I have tried to make it clear that they should not feel responsible if, as is often the case, their loss has been very damaging to them emotionally, physically and psychologically. I believe that the grief experienced by women who have lost children through adoption has for too long been hidden and overlooked, as it was easier for society to believe that they had voluntarily given up their children, had not suffered seriously from their loss and did not deserve sympathy. What I hope that I have made clear in this book is that many women, like me, gave up their children, *in ignorance of the consequences*, as a result of social pressure and fear, that we have, in fact, suffered grievously from the loss of our children and that our suffering and our needs have been grossly underestimated. It is my contention that it was foolish and naive of society to have expected the outcome of losing a child through adoption to have been anything other than very damaging. Because of society's expectations, however, many women have felt guilty and selfish for mourning their lost children and for trying to find them. It is my hope that this book will relieve them of that guilt by making it clear that their reactions are, in fact, the natural, appropriate response to the situation in which they have found themselves. Only when they are given permission by society to grieve can they begin to deal with the loss of their children and go on to take steps towards resolving their grief. Parents who do not raise their own children, for whatever reason, even if those children are never adopted, often experience similar losses.

After presenting my paper in Brisbane, I was approached by several adopted people who told me that my explanation of the nature of adoption-related loss and the concept of disenfranchised grief also helped them to understand their own grief at having been adopted. I hope that I have also shown in this book that adopted people grieve for the loss of their natural mothers and that their grief also has been hidden and denied by society, because it made society feel uncomfortable to have to admit that adoption was not the ideal solution that it was promoted to be. The grief of adopted people is quite legitimate and their losses also need to be acknowledged. Adopted people should not feel guilty for grieving the separation from their original mothers and for trying to find them. This also is a natural, appropriate response to the experience of being adopted. Those who are not raised by their natural parents, for whatever reason, even if they are never actually adopted, often experience similar losses.

I have not addressed the loss experienced by many adoptive parents due to infertility. Since adoption is not a treatment for infertility, I believe that the grief associated with infertility does not belong in a book about adoption. Infertility has been connected with adoption because at one time being infertile was a criterion for being allowed to adopt. Adoption has also been known to cause secondary infertility in women who have lost children through adoption. Some infertile people adopt; others do not. Some adoptive parents are infertile; others are not. While I acknowledge that an adoptive parent's infertility may have an impact on the dynamics and relationships in an adoptive family, infertility itself is *not* an adoption-related loss. I have also not addressed the grief experienced by natural fathers, although I acknowledge that they also suffer from the loss of their children, as do other family members.

My personal experience of adoption spans three decades and three continents. My son was born and adopted in 1970 in Scotland, my homeland, where natural mothers have no legal right to information about their adult, adopted children. In August 1998 I presented a seminar in Edinburgh at the invitation of the British Association of Social Workers. At this seminar I called for changes to Scottish adoption legislation to allow natural parents access to information about their adult, adopted children. I sincerely hope that I live to see those changes come into effect. The beautiful island of Bermuda was also my home for an important period of my life. Since 1982, however, I have lived in South Australia and have been involved in post-adoption services there since 1989. I believe that my book has relevance for anyone, anywhere, whose life has been affected by adoption. Many thousands of adoptions have already taken place around the world. Before we can consider whether or not adoption should have a future, we must explore and try to understand the outcomes for all of those whose lives have already been affected by adoption.

This book is in three parts. Part One, **Mistreated, mateless mother**, is **a** true story of adoption loss. It is my story and my truth. It is written from my perspective as a natural mother. In it I tell my own story of how I lost my first child through adoption and of the impact that loss has had on my life. I describe my feelings and reactions and how they changed over the years. No names have been changed for the purposes of this book and no attempts have been made to preserve anyone's anonymity. This is my experience and I have told it as I experienced it. There have been many fictional accounts of adoption experiences. Few of them bear any resemblance to people's true experiences. I believe that this is because many people feel uncomfortable having the myths about adoption challenged and prefer to read unrealistic accounts, which ignore the real issues. Through my research for the paper which I presented in Brisbane in 1997 (which was published in *Separation, Reunion, Reconciliation*, Proceedings from the Sixth Australian Conference on Adoption, Brisbane, 1997), I discovered that I was not alone in my experience and that many other women had shared similar experiences. My work over a period of years with women who have lost children through adoption has confirmed this.

Part Two of this book, **The grief caused by adoption loss**, is what I believe to be **the** true story of adoption loss and its outcomes. It is written from my perspective as a social worker. In it I explore the literature and research that already exist on adoption loss and grief. Adoption has caused an enormous amount of grief to a great many people. I do not believe that you can have adoption without grief. In this part of the book, I address the effects of adoption on those involved and the reasons why their grief is not easily resolved. I explore ways of healing the pain and discuss the experience of reunion between family members who have been separated by adoption. I believe that this part of the book complements and illuminates the first part, in the same way that the first part illustrates and validates the second part.

In Part Three of this book, **What does it all mean?**, I bring together the issues raised in the first two parts. The first two chapters of this part of the book explore what adoption loss means for me and the second two chapters explore what adoption loss means for society in general. In this part of the book I show how what we can learn from past adoption experiences will lead us towards *a future without adoption*.

Naming of the parties involved with adoption has always been a matter of contention. I feel strongly that it is quite inappropriate and unhelpful to use the term "real" with regard to parents of adopted people. *Each adopted person has four real parents; none of them is imaginary.* The parents who created the child are known as, among other names, genetic parents, biological parents, original parents, birth parents, first parents or natural parents. The parents who have adopted the child into their family are known as, among other names, legal parents, surrogate parents, nurturing parents, social parents or adoptive parents. I have chosen to use the terms "natural" and "adoptive" parents, which I feel are clear and inoffensive terms. I have chosen the term "natural mother" partly because some of the other names cause me some discomfort and partly because pregnancy and childbirth are generally considered to be the way nature intended families to be created. Also, during my research into my family history, I discovered that an illegitimate child in the United Kingdom was traditionally known as a "natural child". As most children who are subsequently adopted are born to single women, the word "natural" seemed appropriate. The terms "natural parent" and "adoptive parent" are the ones used in Australian government legislation, such as The Social Security Act.

I have laboured to produce six offspring in my life - five children and this book. I hope that they will all live on after I am gone as a testimony to my life. I should like to express my gratitude to all those friends and family members who have encouraged and assisted me to write this book.

Part One

Mistreated, mateless mother

Adoption and Loss

Chapter 1 ... in which Evelyn grows up in Renfrew

I was born (towards the end of 1949) and raised in Renfrew, a small, conservative (with a small "c") town on the outskirts of Glasgow, Scotland. The town of Renfrew has been there, on the banks of the River Clyde, since the fourteenth century. Renfrew is part of an industrial, working class area, which expanded, in more recent times, around the shipbuilding industry.

My parents were engaged when the Second World War broke out. My grandmother said to my mother, "You'd better marry him in case he has to go to war. Then if he gets killed you'll get a war widow's pension. If you're not married, you'll get nothing." They married in November 1939 and my father was called up almost immediately. He spent the next six years in Iceland, North Africa and Italy, coming home occasionally on leave and managing thereby to father two children. My mother worked in a munitions factory. The Clyde area was bombed heavily during the war because of the shipyards. In Clydebank, which lies directly across the river from Renfrew, only seven houses were left undamaged after the blitz. When the war ended in 1945, prefabricated homes were built, as they were cheap and easy to erect. My parents moved, with my brother and sister, into a "prefab" and began their life together as a married couple, *six years after their wedding*. My father trained, after the war, as a typewriter mechanic with Remington Rand. Consequently, when I started school I didn't recite "A, B, C, D, E" like the other children. Instead my alphabet began with "Q, W, E, R, T".

Many years later, looking back over his life, my father said to me, "Hitler ruined my life." What he meant was that coming back from the war, he couldn't find his place in society or in his family. The family had grown and developed without him. My mother, like many women at that time, had learned to cope without a man and had been running the household efficiently in his absence. My father, on the other hand, had spent six years taking orders. His children were strangers to him. Returning to his wife and children after the war, he felt redundant.

When I was born, my father had no experience of being a father to a young child. I do not recall spending a great deal of time with my father throughout my childhood. In those days it was not common for fathers to play an active role in their children's upbringing. From my earliest years, my father seemed to resent me. I spent a large part of my life trying to work out why. I remember no hugs, no warmth or affection from my father. In fact, I cannot even remember him using my name to address me. He did address me with various nicknames, however, such as "spewins" and "plouk". At the time, I thought that these were affectionate, pet names. When I was older I learned that they were, in fact, Scottish terms for "vomit" and "pimple" respectively. I do remember that as I was preparing to start school, at the age of four, my father said to me, "No matter what you do, you'll never be as good as your sister or your brother."

As I grew up, I always felt that I was trying, hopelessly, to justify my existence. I didn't seem to be good enough at anything to make any impression on my father. My sister had the advantage of being the first-born and my father thought the world of her. My brother was just the kind of son my father wanted, a soccer player. As a child, I spent a lot of time alone, as my brother and sister were both several years older. They were both at school before I was born. By the time I started primary school, my sister was in high school and by the time I started high school my sister had left home. My brother and sister teased and tormented me constantly, especially my brother. I seemed to have been provided for his entertainment. He loved to jump out on me in the dark and scare me half to death. Another of his favourite pastimes was to hold me down and tickle me until I cried, or hold me at arms' length and slap me, knowing that my arms and legs were too short for me to be able to retaliate. He took delight in swapping the sugar for the salt, so that I ended up with sugar in my soup and salt on my breakfast cereal. In return, when I was old enough, I used to help him train for soccer, spending hours throwing the ball for him and then running to fetch it. When he joined the Boys' Brigade, I polished his drum and his badges. When he stole apples, I let him hide them in my drawer. As a child, I hated him and adored him at the same time.

One of my earliest memories is of being put over my mother's knee and smacked on my bare bottom with a leather belt. I recall my grandmother standing behind my mother telling her to make sure that she hit me hard. My crime? I was playing with the little boy across the road, who was the same age as I was, three years old. He had asked to see my bottom. I was puzzled. I couldn't understand why someone would want to see someone else's bottom. I complied and showed him my bottom, because I didn't know of any reason not to. His mother found us in the garden shed, me with my pants down and sent me home to my grandmother in disgrace. Gran issued the, "Wait until your mother gets home" threat. When Mum came home, Gran insisted that this kind of behaviour had to be nipped in the bud and out came the belt. Down came my pants, yet again, but this time for a quite different purpose. I couldn't understand what I was being punished for. There was no explanation, no discussion. It was obvious to me that I must be a bad person who had done something terribly wrong, otherwise my mother, whom I adored and trusted, would not be beating me. This was not the beginning of a lifetime of physical abuse. In fact, it is the only time I recall being physically punished as a child, but it may have been the start of my confusion and my feelings of worthlessness. Not long after this, I spent two weeks in hospital with scarlet fever. I have a vivid memory of the ambulanceman carrying me in his arms, wrapped in a grey, itchy army blanket, out of our house and into the ambulance. I spent my fourth birthday in hospital, miserable and lonely, believing that I had been removed from my family for my wickedness and would never see them again. After being allowed home, I thought that I had better behave very well so that I wouldn't be taken away from my family again.

My mother worked in my pre-school years and my grandmother looked after me. This was very unusual in the 1950s, a time when it was taken for granted that women with children were full-time carers. The reason that my mother worked, I discovered when I was older, was because my father had an over-fondness for drinking and gambling and my mother had to work to supplement the small and irregular amounts of housekeeping money that he gave her. My mother suffered from a heart condition and had been told by her doctor not to work. She visited him for regular check-ups and lied consistently, denying that she was working. I recall one child very mysteriously telling me that she knew why my mother was the first person in our street to have a washing machine. It was because the doctor had told her that, with her heart condition, she shouldn't be washing by hand. I was terrified. I thought that my mother might die.

My father was always in work, never off sick and never late for work. Every weekend, however, he was blind drunk. I have vivid memories of coming home and finding my father collapsed in a drunken stupor on the front lawn. Sometimes he made it into the house before he collapsed and we would go about our business, carefully stepping over him until he came round. No one was able to lift him. When we found him like this, we would check to see if any change had fallen out of his pockets. We would never have taken money from him, but if it was lying on the floor already, it was anybody's. I became aware as I grew up that the neighbours talked about us. Other children teased me about my father's drinking and about the fact that my mother worked. That made me feel that we were different from other families and, therefore, not quite as good.

Our little community of prefabs was a very safe, friendly one. At least, we felt safe at the time. Environmentally, it was perhaps not the healthiest place to raise children. At one end of our street was the gasworks, at the other end a huge electricity pylon. There were very few cars on the roads in those days and we children played safely in the street, only scattering when the coal truck came or the ragman. The ragman was the highlight of our summer days. We begged for rags from our mothers to trade with the ragman for toys. As a child I read a lot. There were always books in the house, not because my parents bought them, but because, at that time, books were given as awards at school for good results or good attendance. Books were also given at Sunday School and Boys Brigade in recognition of various achievements. I read everything that came into the house and was as interested in *What Katy Did* as I was in what happened down *King Solomon's Mines*. I had plenty of opportunity to read as I was a rather solitary child and I also suffered several bouts of tonsillitis every year, which, in the days when antibiotics were not prescribed, usually lasted about two weeks each. My mother became very frustrated by our doctor who refused to authorise the removal of my tonsils, because they were "perfectly healthy".

I remember my mother as, above all, hospitable and generous. I often came home to find brush salesmen wearing turbans sitting at our kitchen table, eating Mum's home made soup. Mum always had "a wee plate of soup" on hand and offered one to anyone who visited. We lived in the prefab, my sister, brother and I sharing a bedroom, until I was ten years old. Then we moved into a larger house, which we shared with my maternal grandmother.

All through my childhood, although we were poor and had to make do with hand-me-downs, we never missed a summer holiday, thanks to my mother's miraculous budgeting. On one of those exciting holidays, my brother saved my life. My father was, reluctantly, left in charge of the children while Mum went shopping. I was interested in a huge, deep (reputed to be twenty feet) rock pool in which the older children were swimming. While Dad's attention was elsewhere, I accidentally slipped in. I was very small and couldn't swim. My brother managed to grab my arms when I came up for the third time and started to drag me out. What upset me was that he dragged me up the face of the rocks, which tore my legs to shreds. I walked back to the boarding house, soaking wet, shoes squelching, with blood pouring down my legs. Mum was not impressed with Dad's inattention.

The turning point in my relationship with my parents came when I finished primary school. I attended the Blytheswood Testimonial School, not far from our prefab. My academic potential had obviously been spotted at an early stage, as I was accelerated and missed a year, with the result that I completed primary school, after six years instead of seven, at the age of eleven. Because I had done so well, my headmaster, Mr Campbell, was keen for me to take up the opportunity of an academic education. He felt that I had the potential to "make something of myself". My father refused to give permission. His belief was that I should "know my place" and not "get ideas above my station". His plan was to get me out into the workforce as soon as possible. Besides, my sister and brother had not had the advantage of an extended education and so why should I think I deserved any better than they did. I actually had no particular preference at the time. My mother defied him and agreed to send me to Paisley Grammar School, against his wishes. I am sure that he never forgave her or me.

From the time that I started high school, I felt that my father resented everything that I did. He never took any interest in my schoolwork or hobbies and he rarely spoke to me. We communicated through my mother. Home became rather cold and unwelcoming, although my mother did her best for me. I became used to the fact that my father never spoke to me and forgot that there was anything unusual about it. My father seemed determined to interpret everything that I wanted to do as a personal affront to him. All teenagers are rebellious to a certain extent. My rebelliousness took an unusual form. At the age of thirteen I went with some school friends to the Mormon Church (The Church of Jesus Christ of Latter Day Saints) and felt a warmth and approval that had been missing in my life. I had never felt completely accepted at home nor at school but I did feel a valued part of the church community and therein lay the attraction. My father was furious when I started attending church regularly and saying that I would not gamble nor drink alcohol. He seemed to think that it implied that his way of life wasn't good enough for me. When I was fourteen, my father told my mother to tell me that if I went to church once more I needn't bother coming home. I went anyway. I trusted my mother not to let him put me out of the house, but I felt that he'd be happier if I weren't there.

My teenage rebellion also involved trying to make a difference in the world. I joined the Campaign for Nuclear Disarmament (CND). My father objected to that too, of course and tried to put a stop to my involvement, not by talking to me about it, but by destroying all my posters and literature while I was out. He complained when I became involved in bread-and-cheese lunches to raise money for starving children in Africa and went door-to-door collecting money for Oxfam. He seemed to look for ways to spoil things for me. I really enjoyed playing the piano. My father's sister had been a piano teacher and I had had lessons from the ages of eight to thirteen. We had a huge, diverse collection of music as we had all of my aunt's music as well as my sister's and mine. One day, when I was about fourteen, I came home from school and the piano was gone. There had been no warning, no discussion. My father had decided to give our piano away. It was my grandmother's piano (my father's mother) and I had assumed that it would stay in the family. I had had hopes of one day having it in my own home. The piano stool with all the music was gone too. I asked my mother, "Where did Dad put the music?" Mum asked Dad. Dad said that he had given away the piano and the stool. The music was included. I found out where the piano was (the local bowling club) and explained to them that my father had inadvertently given away all of our music, much of which had sentimental value and could I please have it back again. They refused to have any dealings with me, as my father had been the one to make the arrangements. My father refused to discuss the matter of the music with them and so it was gone forever. I felt that he did it deliberately to make me unhappy. I was always puzzled by my father's meanness to me.

I was so convinced by my family that I didn't deserve anything, that when, in my third year of high school, the

9

opportunity came through the school to go on a Mediterranean cruise, I passed it up. I didn't even ask at home if I could go, because I was constantly being reminded that I was costing the family money by staying on in school and that I should be out earning money to pay my way. When my mother found out about the cruise, she asked if I would like to go. I pretended that I didn't want to go because I knew that if I went my father would resent it and never let me forget it. I decided that the emotional cost was too high. My brother even offered to pay some of the cost himself, but I still refused because I always felt obligated to the family, as if I were depriving them just by existing. All of my friends went on the cruise, every one of them. They sent me postcards and brought me gifts. I had to attend school as usual. There was another school cruise when I was in my sixth year. Again, I studied while my friends travelled.

The atmosphere at home was becoming more and more like a battleground and I was feeling less and less welcome there. From the age of fifteen, I was the only child left at home. When I was sixteen and in my exam year at high school, my sister, who was married and living in Bermuda, had her first child and asked my mother to go to Bermuda to help her out. My mother went on what was planned to be a three-week holiday, but ended up staying three months. I was left behind to look after my father, although my grandmother did some of the cooking. Every weekend Dad would give me the housekeeping money and I had to do all the shopping and pay the bills. I remember struggling up the High Street in Renfrew with several bags of shopping in the pouring rain. The rain soaked the bags (which were made of paper in those days, not plastic) and the bags broke and the contents of my shopping bags went rolling down the street. I ran after them, tucking oranges in my pockets and tins of soup under my arms and headed for home, drenched and frustrated. I often had to ask him for more money in the middle of the week, which made him very angry. "Your mother never asks for more", he bellowed at me. My mother must have been a financial genius. Finally I had to beg my mother to come home as my higher exams (Scottish Certificate of Education) were about to start and I was

10

finding it hard to study. In those days everything depended on your final exams, there was no continuous assessment. Mum arrived back just before my exams started.

Paisley Grammar School was founded in 1586 and had a proud tradition of providing a quality education. I spent six years there, but, coming from a working class background, I always felt out of place. In spite of that, I worked hard to make the most of the opportunity. I will be forever grateful to my mother for her willingness to give me that opportunity and for accepting me always for myself. In those days employment training had made no insidious inroads into schools. Education was provided for its own sake, not as a means to obtaining employment. Real education teaches young people to think and to feel. Education has a civilising influence on society and produces young adults who have learned analytical thinking and empathy, qualities of which one can never have enough.

We were actually told that, as students at a grammar school, we were "a cut above the rest". I felt more like a cut below the rest. I worked hard at school because I enjoyed learning. I never did fit in, though. I was never a model student, I'm delighted to say. The fact is, I never wanted to fit in. They had a rule in Paisley Grammar that at the end of your exam year, when the final exams were over, you could leave school before the end of term, if you had a job. My brother and sister had both left school and joined the workforce when they were fifteen. Because I stayed on at school past that age, I was always made to feel like a freeloader at home. In order to contribute something and pay my way to some degree, I had worked part-time since I was fifteen years old. I worked weekends and school holidays in a baker's shop. As soon as I could, therefore, I was out of school and back behind the counter at the City Bakeries. The other part to the rule was that if you did leave school before the end of term to work, you weren't allowed to attend the final school dance. I think that rule was designed to keep us working class children in our place, because, of course, most of the students were not under any pressure from their parents to earn money. I decided to go to the school dance anyway, as I thought that the rule was discriminatory and unfair. The Deputy Headmistress escorted me ignominiously to the door as soon as I was spotted.

After my higher exams, in my fifth year of high school, I was the top student in French and was awarded the French prize (*Les Miserables* by Victor Hugo, in French). My parents didn't come to the prize giving, of course. I have a vivid memory of obtaining my Scottish Certificate of Education higher results and sharing them with my mother. Against all odds I did remarkably well. Mum congratulated me on my achievement and encouraged me to show them to my father. I was reluctant but she was confident that he would be proud of me. I was persuaded to present my results to him. His only comment was, "Was that the best you could do?" I felt quite deflated. I learned from that experience never to hope for my father's approval again. Hitler may have ruined his life, but it seemed to be me that he took his revenge on.

Chapter 2 ... in which Evelyn moves to Edinburgh

I had no idea what I was going to do when I left school. Some of my friends were going to university. I assumed that we couldn't afford it. Then a friend told me that it didn't cost anything. I knew that my parents wanted me out in the workforce, earning money, but I thought that I'd like to try to further my education. I asked Mum if I could go to university. Mum said Dad would never allow it. We went through the same upheaval that we had when I had left primary school. My father was against the idea, of course. Some fathers would have been proud of a child who was offered a place at university, but my father interpreted it as yet another rejection of his way of life. No one in my family had attended university since my great-great-grandfather, who was a lawyer and the illegitimate son of a baronet. As I was only seventeen, I required my parents' permission. My father refused to sign his name and so my mother forged his signature.

I was offered places at Glasgow, Edinburgh and Manchester universities. I decided not to go to Glasgow University as I felt that it would not be much different from being at school, living with my parents and associating with the people that I had gone to school with. That would have been "playing it safe". I decided instead that the time had come for me to leave home. I was keen to leave as I was tired of always feeling criticised there. I was also keen to leave Renfrew. My one aim was to have an interesting life and I didn't think that would happen if I stayed in

Renfrew. I wanted to take chances, to be adventurous. I didn't want my life to be predictable, which I thought it would be if I stayed in Renfrew. I chose to go to Edinburgh University, which meant not only moving out of home but also leaving everything that was familiar. I left family dramas behind me for the big, wide world of academia. The idea scared me, but excited me too.

I had only ever visited Edinburgh once before, when I was very small, when my family and I flew from Renfrew Airport to Edinburgh for a day trip. I arrived in Edinburgh in 1967, with nowhere to stay and no idea even where the university was. At the age of seventeen I suddenly had to deal with landlords (sometimes crazy), bills and budgeting, as well as finding my way around in a strange place. I grew to love the city of Edinburgh in the three years that I lived there. I loved its grandeur and its history. Geographically Edinburgh is about fifty miles from Renfrew, but it felt like the other side of the world. No one in the family had a telephone or a car and so there was little communication. During the first year I spent in Edinburgh, I often went home at weekends, to meet up with old friends, often hitchhiking, as I couldn't afford the train fare.

Moving away from home also meant the end of a promising relationship. I had been seeing my boyfriend for two years and if I hadn't moved away we would probably have married. After I moved to Edinburgh he visited me several times, in an attempt to renew the relationship. It was too late for me. I had embarked on a new and exciting life and felt that I had left him behind. Finally he came to visit unexpectedly one evening. We had another unexpected visitor there, the brother of a friend, who had come looking for her. I had never met him before. He was in his thirties, from London, sophisticated and mature. I said that he could spend the night at our flat as he had travelled up from London looking for his sister and had nowhere else to stay. My ex-boyfriend arrived and I was concerned that we were in for another night of exhausting introspection and pointless raking over of the past. I surreptitiously asked my friend's brother if he would pretend to be my boyfriend, thinking that that would cut short the visit of my ex-boyfriend. Unfortunately, as he moved in quite different circles from those that I moved in, he took his role-play a little too far. When my ex-boyfriend showed no signs of leaving, my friend's brother stood up, walked to the bedroom door and before he entered it, turned to me and said, "I'm going to bed now, dear - don't be long." I don't know who was more dumbfounded, my ex-boyfriend or I. In the two years that we had been going out together, we had not had a sexual relationship. This was not uncommon at the time. We had planned to wait until we were married to have sex. I didn't know what to do. I felt trapped. If I explained that I'd never met this man until about two hours before then I would expose my little deceit. I kept quiet. My ex-boyfriend was terribly upset and left. I didn't see him again for twenty-two years, when I finally confessed to him. We enjoyed a very romantic, although brief, reunion and old hurts were healed.

At the end of my first year at university, when I was eighteen, my sister asked my parents to move to Bermuda, where she was living. My mother was unsure about going, as she felt guilty about leaving me. I encouraged them to go as I felt that it was too great an opportunity to miss. My parents were fifty years old and it was a big step for them. My mother had already visited Bermuda but my father had never been there. It took a lot of courage for them to make that move. My brother, by this time, was living in South Africa, having been offered a contract there as a professional soccer player. Mum and Dad went to live in Bermuda and from then on I felt that I had no home at all, even an unwelcoming one.

I can't say that I really enjoyed university. Although government grants had made it easier for working class young people to attend university, I mostly felt like a fish out of water there. I did enjoy the time I spent in Edinburgh, but not necessarily the time I spent at university. In many ways the late 1960s was a wonderful time to be young. It was a time of hope and optimism. Music was everything. We enjoyed many live concerts, Jimi Hendrix (for whom the word "charisma" could have been invented), Bob Dylan, Pink Floyd, Cream. Books were important too, of course. We read Tolkien, Kerouac, Henry Miller and Lawrence Durrell and dreamed of travelling and meeting interesting people. But social issues counted too; it wasn't all fun and games. Martin Luther King Jr had a dream and we all shared it.

At the end of my first year of university, I spent an enjoyable summer working as a chambermaid on the Isle of Wight, while I considered whether or not I wanted to continue my studies. I met some great characters there, young people who were passing the summer months, sleeping on the beaches and in parks. I used to save leftovers from the hotel to feed them, as they had no money. They asked me to go to London with them and I seriously considered it, but finally declined. I attended Britain's first ever three-day rock festival on the Isle of Wight and mingled with crowds of peaceful, excited young people watching Arthur Brown, Tyrannosaurus Rex and Jefferson Airplane. Life was easy. While I made beds and cleaned toilets I awaited my results and wondered where my future lay. I decided that if I had passed all of my subjects then I would continue with my degree, because that would mean that I was capable and so it would be a waste not to go on. If I failed anything at all, then I wouldn't resit or repeat, I would leave university and make other plans. In fact, I passed with flying colours and so I felt obliged to complete my degree, but it was touch and go. I returned to the ancient, empty streets of Edinburgh after the summer. I studied hard and had good friends and managed without my family.

Shortly after arriving in Edinburgh, I had met Marie, a student Nursery Nurse (Child Care Worker) from Middlesborough, in the north of England and shared accommodation with her for most of the time that I lived there. When I returned to Edinburgh from the Isle of Wight, we rented a small one-bedroomed flat. It had a little gas fire in the living room, but no heating in the bedroom. We regularly slept wearing hats and scarves and woke up to ice on the windows - on the inside as well as the outside. Edinburgh is a very cold city in the winter. We had no television, only a little transistor radio and Marie's valued record player (mono, of course). We decorated the walls of our flat with articles from International Times and Oz magazine. We didn't have proper beds, only mattresses on the floor. I had "binned" mine, that is I stole it from the edge of the street where someone had put it out to be collected by the rubbish truck. That was how we furnished the flat. I remember one night we were walking home from one of our expeditions carrying a dining chair each and a police car drove past. We felt so guilty that we instinctively put the chairs down where we were and sat on them. Perhaps we thought that it made us look less conspicuous.

I did spend that first Christmas with my parents in Bermuda. I had just turned eighteen and travelled on a student charter flight to New York. Because of the timing of the charter, I was unable to get a flight to Bermuda the same day. I had to spend the night in New York. So there I was, eighteen years old and the furthest I had been from Renfrew was Edinburgh. I had very little money and no idea where I was going to spend the night. I asked at the information desk at the airport. They suggested the Airport Hotel but it was too expensive. They rang the YWCA for me but they were full. Finally they booked me into a hotel in Times Square. I found out where the buses left from and somehow, at night, alone in New York, found my way to Times Square, not realising that it was a very seedy part of town. I found the hotel that I was booked into, the Woodstock; it cost $8.00 a night. I didn't like the look of it, but it seemed that I had no choice. I paid my money, got my room key and headed for the lift. Three middle-aged men followed me into the lift. They looked as if they had walked out of a Humphrey Bogart movie, short and stocky with coat collars turned up and hats low over their eyes. I wondered if they were carrying guns. I got off at the first floor just to get away from them and walked the rest of the way to my room, rushed inside and locked the door. I was jet-lagged and also fascinated by all-night American TV. Combined with these factors, I was too afraid to sleep and so I watched the sun come up over Manhattan as the rubbish trucks rumbled through the city. I visited New York many times in the next few years, but I never forgot my first brave foray into the heart of the city.

As we flew across the Atlantic towards Bermuda, the captain announced, "We are now beginning our descent to Bermuda." I was astounded and thought that he must have made a mistake, as there was no sign of land. When I did finally spot Bermuda it looked too small to even land an aeroplane on. In fact it is only one and a half miles wide at its widest point. My mother was the matron of a nursing home there and lived on the premises. I spent a few weeks there, helping her with the residents and then returned to Edinburgh in the New Year to continue my studies. I had no idea what the future held, but I had decided to get an education and had hopes for a productive and happy life. Little did I know that my dreams were about to be shattered.

Chapter 3 ... in which Evelyn falls in love

This was a time when sex education didn't exist, either at home or at school and the expectation was that people did not have sex unless they were married. My plan, as a teenager, was to do just that, wait until I was married before I had sex. However, at the end of 1967, I had finally met a young man whom I had admired from afar for some time. Over the next eighteen months, we conducted an odd sort of relationship, which was a combination of friendship and romance. He had travelled to the Isle of Wight while I was there in 1968 and spent some time with me there. In fact, we attended the Isle of Wight festival together. We lived a long way apart, but we visited, wrote letters, exchanged gifts and grew very fond of each other. Early in 1969, he decided to do what many young people were doing at that time, travel around Europe, hitch-hiking, looking for work, exploring. I missed him terribly. He wrote me long, descriptive letters telling me of his adventures and that he missed me. He wrote me simple, romantic poems ("The wind blows, The grass grows, And the world knows, This love never ends."). I longed for his return. At this stage in my life I had been living independently of my parents for nearly two years, but I had never smoked, never drunk alcohol and never had sex. In many ways I was still very innocent and idealistic.

I was awakened one night in June, at about midnight, by a knock at the door. There he stood. He told me that he had just returned from across the English Channel and had wanted to

19

come straight to my house, but was unable to get a lift in my direction. Instead he had gone to his mother's, left his luggage and then come straight to me. That made me feel very special. I adored him. I was so happy that he had come back to me. We sat and talked. He told me about his travels and said that he now wanted to stay in one place for a while and asked could he move into our flat. I was sharing with Marie at the time, but the obvious implication was that we would be "living together". I thought that all of my dreams had come true. He didn't actually make any promises, but he did lead me to believe that I meant a lot to him. I trusted him completely. I had been listening to Bob Dylan singing, "Why wait any longer for the one you love, when he's standing in front of you?" Next minute I had opened the door and there he was. I loved him and wanted to spend my life with him. That night we were lovers for the first time. I'm sure that he knew that it was my first time. We never talked about contraception. As we were going to be living together, I planned to try to go on the pill. It was difficult as most doctors would only prescribe it for married women (and sometimes only with their husbands' permission), but I thought that I could find a way.

Although we had been seeing each other for some time, the sexual relationship was very spontaneous and unplanned. With hindsight, I am very glad that my first sexual experience was with someone that I loved dearly and with whom I wanted to spend my life. Apparently people were walking on the moon about then, but that didn't really interest me, as I was already on cloud nine. Neil Armstrong might have been taking small steps, but I had just taken my own personal giant leap. I had hopes of a lasting relationship, which would eventually lead to marriage. He spent a few days making enquiries about jobs in our area and then said that he needed to go back to his mother's home to collect the rest of his belongings.

He never came back.

The fact that he walked out on me, without a word of explanation, within a few days of our first sexual experience together, was very damaging to the impressionable and uncertain young woman that I was. I felt emotionally bruised and battered, shocked, discarded, saddened, confused and disappointed all at once. He showed no inclination to discuss our relationship and appeared instead to have suddenly resumed a previous relationship. I was devastated by what I perceived as his treachery. It was not only a private humiliation but also a public one as many of our friends knew of our plans and it was very embarrassing to be so summarily thrown aside. My self-esteem was at rock bottom. I wondered what I had done wrong. I felt worthless. The worst thing was that I realised that I had trusted him and obviously misjudged him. I blamed myself for that. I felt gullible and disappointed in myself and thought that I should have known better. At the time, I was too sad to be angry. Anger came later. I felt naive and stupid. I felt used.

I went to stay with my parents in Bermuda on a working holiday to get away from it all and nurse my broken heart. Bermuda is the most beautiful place that I have ever visited. When I disembarked there in the summer of 1969, I thought that I had walked into an oven. I had never experienced such heat in Scotland. Bermuda has the cleanest, clearest, warmest, bluest ocean water of anywhere in the world. There is no pollution. The climate is almost perfect; not too hot in summer and not too cold in winter. The air is clean, the beaches are clean, the flowers are glorious and the people are warm and hospitable. In spite of all of these distractions, I thought about him all the time. The local young men didn't interest me as my heart was still elsewhere. Towards the end of my two months there, I found out that another Isle of Wight concert had been arranged and that Bob Dylan (my all-time favourite singer/songwriter) was going to be playing. I desperately wanted to be back in Britain to attend the concert, but I was booked on a student charter flight again and when I rang them they said that it wasn't possible to change flights. I rang again and told them that my grandmother was dying and I had to get back urgently. They were very sympathetic and said that they would do what they could. They finally rang me back with the great news that they had managed to change my flight. The one that they had moved me on to arrived in London the day after the Isle of Wight concert finished. I said, "It's all right, she's much better now" and resigned myself to missing it. If I had managed to get on an earlier flight, what happened next might not have happened at all.

I was on the beach one Saturday afternoon, towards the end of my stay there, when I heard someone call my name. I looked around to see a tanned, handsome young man. "Do I know you?" He said that he was a friend of someone who knew me and had asked and found out my name. We walked along the beach and talked. He asked why he never saw me with a boyfriend. I replied that I wasn't interested in boyfriends. "Aha", he said perceptively, "someone has hurt you badly." He encouraged me to tell him the sad story of my doomed love affair. He was very sympathetic, told me that I was charming and attractive and that, "That guy must be crazy to treat you like that." He begged me not to judge all men harshly because of one unhappy experience. I was flattered, of course. We arranged to meet at a club that evening.

In the evening he was friendly and attentive. We left the club in the early hours of the morning. He offered me a ride home on his motor bike. We set off in the warm, fragrant Bermuda night. He wanted to stop to show me a particularly beautiful, waterfront park. We walked around the park for a while, enjoying the view. We sat down. We kissed and cuddled. Next thing I knew he was undressing.

I said, "What are you doing?"

He replied, "Don't worry it's all right."

I began to panic. There was no one around, of course. I didn't know exactly where I was, nor how to get home from there, but I knew that it was a long way.

"Please take me home now", I pleaded.

"Not yet", he replied.

All of a sudden it sounded very sinister. What followed was a lot of struggling and wriggling, but no actual violence. It was all over very quickly. I was so naive and inexperienced that I wasn't even sure afterwards whether the sex act had actually been completed or not. All I knew was that I wanted to go home and somehow I felt that I had more chance of getting home safely with him, than if I had run off into the unknown Bermuda night all by myself. All I could think of while all of this was going on was that I had got it wrong again, that I was obviously very stupid and a very poor judge of character still. Afterwards he didn't even take me home. He drove me to where I could get a taxi, with the excuse that he didn't have enough petrol. I felt used yet again. The expression "date-rape" didn't exist in those days. Had I been asked, I wouldn't have described my experience as a rape. Rape in the 1960s involved violence and force. I know that if I hadn't already lost my virginity, I would have resisted more strenuously. I was intimidated and in a position of weakness and he took advantage of that. I was angry and disillusioned after our brief encounter, with him, with my first lover and with myself. I not only felt used, I felt soiled and spoiled. I didn't talk to anyone about it. I thought that perhaps if I didn't speak about it that I could pretend that it had never happened. I went home in a taxi, had a shower and hoped that I would never see him again. I didn't.

Back in Edinburgh, four weeks later, I discovered that I was pregnant.

To say that I was shocked and dismayed does not even begin to come close to describing my reaction to the news. I was devastated. I received the results of my pregnancy test from the doctor at the Student Health Service. As I sat in the waiting room before my appointment, I was suddenly gripped by excruciating stomach cramps. I was unable to move. I didn't know what to do. Should I call out for help? I didn't understand what was happening to me. I knew that if my name were called I should be unable to respond. Looking back now, I think that I was gripped by a very physical fear of what I was about to hear. The doctor was very unsympathetic and world-weary. After giving me the news that my pregnancy test was positive (I didn't even understand what he meant, were they positive that I was pregnant or positive that I wasn't?), he dismissed me to "go away and think about it" and come back in a few weeks. I left the surgery in tears, wandered the streets, literally not knowing where I was going.

Finally, exhausted from my wandering, I found myself by a telephone box and rang Marie, who was at work, awaiting the news. She was the first person that I told. Then I found my way home and howled continuously, alone, for hours out of sheer misery. I was still a Christian at the time, which was why I had postponed having a sexual relationship until I thought that I had found the man with whom I wanted to spend my life. Because of this, the fact of my pregnancy came as even more of a shock. I blamed both of my sex partners for the pregnancy, but most of all I blamed myself for having been taken in and used by both of them.

Then I remembered that I had to have an X-ray. At that time, students had a chest X-ray at the beginning of each academic year. I had arranged to go with a friend. I had had no time to even consider the implications of my pregnancy and so I was going through the motions of my "normal" life. I turned up for my X-ray, gave my name and student number, and proceeded into the X-ray room. Suddenly I caught sight of a sign, "If you are pregnant or think you may be pregnant, please inform the nurse". I panicked. I realised that I was pregnant. I had no idea why the nurse needed to know but I felt obliged to obey the instruction. I had only had a few hours to get used to the idea that I was pregnant and I had only told one person so far and so it was very hard for me to whisper it guiltily to this cold, efficient nurse. She immediately bustled me back out, "You can't have an X-ray." I was sent back to the front desk, as my name had to be taken off the list. The woman behind the desk was furious with me for ruining her list and putting her numbers out of sequence. I slunk off, very embarrassed.

The only slim hope, to which I clung like a life raft, was that conception might have occurred before I went to Bermuda. I went back to my doctor and asked him, in desperation, if it was possible that my pregnancy was two months more advanced than he had thought. My naive question only seemed to confirm what he already believed, that I was promiscuous and stupid. It was vital to me to know who the father of my child was. I knew from the start that if my first lover had been the father of the child that I was carrying, then nothing in the world would have made me part with his baby. I still loved him, although I had been badly damaged emotionally by the way he had treated me so cruelly. I was assured, however, that I had only recently become pregnant. My hopes were dashed. I also realised that once he knew that I was pregnant to someone else, there was certainly no hope of a reconciliation. Once I was sure how and when conception had occurred, I felt that I could never love this child, as I had never loved his father. I was horrified at the thought that a child had been created by that sordid, unpleasant experience. I wrote to my child's father, to tell him that I was pregnant. I wrote to his place of employment, as I didn't know his home address. I never received an answer. I discovered the following year that he had left Bermuda shortly after I did. I don't know if he ever got my letter.

Abortion became legal in Scotland in 1967. Doctors could only approve the termination of a pregnancy, however, if there were medical grounds. I asked my doctor if I could get an abortion. He told me that he could only approve an abortion if my health was at risk. I told him that I felt as if I was going crazy. He frowned, sighed with contempt and said, "There is no medical reason why you should not continue with this pregnancy." I asked for a second opinion. He sent me to another doctor who said exactly the same thing. I had heard of illegal abortions, but I had no idea how to make enquiries about such a thing. I also had no money at all to pay for it. I was too afraid to do anything risky in case it would harm my baby. It looked as if I was going to have to go ahead with my pregnancy. An unmarried woman who was pregnant in the 1960s was described as being "in trouble". That was me, well and truly in trouble.

Chapter 4 ... in which Evelyn announces her news

The members of my immediate family, including my parents, were all living overseas. I wrote to my mother to give her the news. My mother wrote back asking how and when it had happened and what was I going to do about it. I have no idea what my father's reaction to my pregnancy was, but I could guess. I suppose my pregnancy confirmed what he had always thought about me, that I was somehow second rate. It certainly confirmed my low opinion of myself. It was ironic that people had thought that I might "go off the rails" because I moved away from home at the age of seventeen, yet I actually became pregnant while I was living (temporarily) with my parents. The time came when I felt that I had to announce my pregnancy to the world in general. I have a few memories of breaking the news to people, of their reactions, mostly baffled and discomfited. No one congratulated. Some commiserated. I discovered years later, talking to old friends, that some of them had asked me about my child's father, but that I had refused to discuss his identity. As a result of my reticence, they were left to speculate. I felt so guilty about how I had become pregnant. I blamed myself because I had consented to sex the first time and I felt that my pregnancy was an indirect result of that decision on my part, even although I had not consented to the sex that had actually led to the pregnancy. I did not describe what had happened as a rape. It is much easier to recognise rape when there is violence or the threat of violence. Looking back, I realise that my anger probably was expressed in what may have appeared to some to be an off-hand attitude. In fact, I was not only angry about my pregnancy, I was also terrified. I made it very clear to people that I did not want this child. My close friends accepted my predicament without judgment. Others were not so generous. Many people said that they were disappointed in me and that I had let them down, that I had let myself down.

I had to decide what I was going to do. Would I try to finish university or give up? Would I take some time off and come back afterwards? Many people thought that I should leave university and go to live with my parents. I didn't even consider that. Although my father was three thousand miles away, I could feel his disapproval emanating from across the ocean. I certainly didn't want to live with it on a daily basis. I felt that one tragedy was enough. Abandoning my education would be yet another disaster. I thought about Mr Campbell, my primary school headmaster and his plans for me to "make something of myself" and I decided that I couldn't just give up, just because of this setback. I felt that at least I could do something to be proud of, finish my degree. I did, however, withdraw from the two extra subjects in which I had enrolled. Those would have given me a better qualification, but I felt that I would do well if I could just complete the bare minimum of subjects in order to graduate.

There were, throughout my pregnancy and the subsequent adoption process, many hurts and insults. There were many people who moralised, who judged and who felt justified in punishing me. The most common form of punishment was to isolate me socially. As soon as my pregnancy became known, I was regarded by many, suddenly, as a second-class human being. Some people just looked away when they saw me coming and didn't speak. The most painful situation I had to cope with was the number of people who, although they had known me for many years, now made assumptions about me, simply because I was pregnant. The most prevalent assumption was that because I had become pregnant, I must be promiscuous and probably had been for a long time. To my horror, people even asked me if this was my first pregnancy. I was also shocked to be asked if I knew who the baby's father was. I not only knew who his father was, I knew the exact date that he was conceived. Considering this occurred on what was virtually my second sexual experience, it was not too difficult to calculate. One church member, on hearing the news, asked me, "What have you done to yourself now?", as if I had acted alone in the matter. That was typical of people's attitudes, not just in the church, but in the community in general. Being pregnant was my fault entirely. I was responsible. No one was interested in how or why it had happened. No one blamed the child's father. I had "got myself into trouble" - a miracle conception. I was very hurt that people regarded me as a quite different person as soon as they became aware that I was pregnant, especially when these attitudes came from my Christian friends. It seemed that nothing else that I had done, nothing that I had been was relevant any more. Everything was overshadowed by the fact that I was single and pregnant. People avoided me as if my wickedness might be contagious. I suddenly became defined by my reproductive condition. By announcing my pregnancy, I had offered myself up on the sacrificial altar of their self-righteousness. Their attitudes made me even angrier and inclined to respond resentfully, as I had no emotional resources with which to combat their judgmental assumptions.

Deep inside I was seething with rage. It seemed that I had lost all right to be treated with sensitivity and compassion. I was angry at the people who looked down on me and I was even angry at the people who were trying to help, because I felt that nothing they could do could make matters any better. Some friends did try to help and I appreciated their efforts. In spite of anything they could do, however, I felt as if my life were over. I was angry at life for dealing me what seemed at the time to be a fatal blow. It appeared to me to be the death of my hopes and plans for the future.

In my early teenage years I had come to understand that people did not always have children by choice. Suddenly I was able to make sense of what my father had told me, that he only ever wanted two children. I was his third (and last). I understood then, that I was a "mistake", the result of an unplanned

28

pregnancy. My father had also told me that when my mother announced that she was pregnant with me, his response had been a resounding, "Oh, no!" He followed that, apparently with, "Well at least it won't be too bad if it's a boy." It was me. I finally began to realise why I felt unwelcomed by my father. I was afraid that if I kept my child, my anger at my pregnancy and with my child's father would lead me to make my child feel unwelcome also and so I decided that he deserved better than that and that there would be people who would not have my feelings of anger and would be able to make him welcome in their life. I wanted his home life to be warm and nurturing, not cold and adversarial, as mine often had been. Adoption seemed the only way to fulfil the obligation I felt I had towards this "unwelcome" child who had been unwittingly created.

My church was telling me that there was only one way to atone for my sin and that was to give my child to a worthy, married couple. According to the church, they deserved him and I didn't. It was obvious to them from the fact that I was unmarried and pregnant that I was not a person who would be a good mother. The church had been good to me in many ways. Church members had made me feel welcome when I hadn't felt welcome at home. I trusted the church completely. At this point I was still very tied up with the church on an emotional level. I was prepared to agree to whatever the church leaders demanded of me because I was so anxious to try to win back their approval, which had been so crucial to my adolescent development. Because I was feeling so guilty and unworthy, I accepted everything that they said and the church found a suitable couple and told them that they could have my child. I believed that they would not know his history, that they would welcome him unconditionally. I realised that regardless of who was responsible for this situation, my unborn child was quite innocent, and, as such, deserved the best. I believed that I would be unable to give him what he deserved.

I recall my first visit to the maternity hospital. I saw a sign, which read, "All unmarried women must see the almoner". I realised, with a shock, that this referred to me. So cowed was I, that I did not even consider not obeying this instruction. I made an appointment to see the hospital almoner and told her that the church was arranging an adoption. In those days private adoptions were still legal. I remember the almoner as prim, middle-aged and distant. I resented what I perceived as her attempts to intrude. I didn't want to answer any of her questions. I felt that it was not her business. I thought that I had no choice but to submit myself to her cross-examination, but I complied as little as possible. I resigned myself to the fact that she was only doing her job. Her job, as I saw it, was to help to arrange the adoption. I never thought of her as a support person and I never considered confiding in her. As far as I was concerned she was never on my side. When she asked about my child's father, however, I lied. I lied to her for two reasons. First of all, I was too embarrassed to tell her how I had become pregnant. I still blamed myself. At that time young women were expected to be in control of men's sexual behaviour as well as their own. "Nice girls" said "No". What did "nice boys" do, I wonder. Secondly, I lied because I had been feeling so used and so powerless for so long that it was my one little opportunity to exercise my control. I invented a mythical boyfriend who loved me deeply. He was a student, but just not ready for commitment. I lied to try to make my situation seem a little more respectable. After that first visit, I don't think I saw the almoner again until after my child was born, but the lies and the secrets had started already.

I never felt that the child that I was carrying was *my* child. It was, in the beginning, *his* child. I did not believe that I could ever come to love *his* child because I hated *him*. Once the adoption had been arranged, which happened very early in the pregnancy, from being *his* child, my unborn child was then transformed into *their* child. Many years later I read Joss Shawyer's book, *Death by Adoption*, in which a woman who has given up a child for adoption says that she didn't give away *her* baby, because by the time the adoption took place, the baby was no longer hers, her baby had "died" already. That was how I felt.

I thought that I was being sensible and responsible by putting my child's welfare first. I only discovered later that it was all a trick. It was like what they used to do to women who were suspected of being witches. They threw them over a waterfall in a barrel. If they survived, then that proved that they were, in fact, witches and they were then burned at the stake. If they didn't survive, then that proved that they were innocent - but dead, of course. In my case, they told me that if I loved my baby I would give him away to a better life. Then after I did give him up they told me that that proved that I didn't really love him after all, because if I had loved him I could never have parted with him, in spite of what everyone had said.

Chapter 5 ... in which Evelyn thinks things over

Adoption seemed the reasonable, logical answer, but I knew in my heart that it wasn't right. It wasn't the way it should be. My fear of raising a child that I couldn't love unconditionally, coupled with my childhood memories of not feeling accepted by my father, kept me to my plan. To this day my initial, brief reaction to the news of a pregnancy is a sinking feeling in my stomach. The nightmare of my first pregnancy, I feel, will never quite leave me. I felt very let down by life. I felt betrayed. My dreams and hopes for the future were shattered. My plans to "make something of myself" seemed to be in tatters. Somewhere deep inside me, I knew from the moment that my pregnancy was confirmed, that my life would never be the same again.

My feelings towards my pregnancy and my feelings towards my child were always quite separate. I hated the fact that I was pregnant. I was furious that this unwanted obligation had been forced upon me. I hated my child's father. I hated my first lover for making love to me and then abandoning me. I hated myself, because I believed that I had been gullible and stupid and was therefore responsible for all my problems. But I never, at any time, hated my unborn child. I felt no emotion for the little stranger who was growing inside me. I did not think that I had any love to offer this little intruder. I felt only obligation. I was very aware that this innocent child was totally dependent on me for his welfare and I was very protective of him. I was very conscientious about medical matters in order not to disadvantage him in any way. I made sure that I took my vitamins regularly and attended for medical check-ups when told to. In fact, after I had shocked everyone with the announcement of my pregnancy, I dropped my rebellious attitude and adopted one of compliance and apology. I felt guilty and responsible and believed that all I could do was to try somehow to compensate for what I perceived to be my mistakes and errors of judgment. I believed that I had caused this dreadful situation, that I had created this awful problem and that I was inconveniencing everyone else who was concerned.

I resented everyone else in the world who didn't have this burden, this responsibility that had been thrust upon me like a thunderbolt out of the blue. It was all so unfair. My anger simmered all through my pregnancy. Looking back, I realise that there were times when I took out this anger on those close to me. It wasn't them I was angry with, it was myself and my situation. I have few memories of being pregnant. I think this is because I spent the whole time in denial, pretending that it wasn't happening. I felt defeated, as if I couldn't win. Life was conspiring against me. And, yes, I did consider suicide. Again, I was afraid of not succeeding and harming my unborn child. I felt that my life had been ruined by my pregnancy and hoped that I would die in childbirth. Death seemed like the only escape from this impossible dilemma. I felt that I was in a no-win situation. I was afraid to keep my child as I didn't want him to be raised to feel that he was a "mistake", as I was (in 1969, I don't believe that anyone deliberately had a child out of wedlock and so being illegitimate made it clear that a child was unplanned) and I was afraid to give him up as I didn't know how I could live with myself afterwards. My biggest fear was that I wouldn't be able to love him, that every time I looked at him I would be reminded of how he came to be. I felt that he deserved to be loved and I didn't think that I could give him what he deserved. But I also had the fear that if I did give him away, I would hate myself, and worse, that my child would hate me.

At the beginning of my third year at university, Marie and I were sharing a miserable, cramped, little one-bedroomed flat, two flights up in a very old tenement building in St Leonards Street (now the site of the Divisional Police Headquarters). We had no bathroom (only the kitchen sink) and shared a toilet with the neighbours. I had no idea how I could provide for a child. I lived on a student grant, which kept me just below the poverty line. I had to work in the Christmas and summer holidays to keep my head above water. My grant was reduced because my parents were both working. The government expected my parents to contribute something towards supporting me, but they refused. I was barely managing to support myself. I was in my third year of university and had no idea if, or when, I would get a job, or even what kind of work I might do. A degree in Biblical Studies and French isn't terribly useful when it comes to competing for jobs. People said afterwards how well I had done to complete my degree. What I remember most about my final year is walking through Edinburgh with my head down, dejected but not quite defeated. I thought about my pregnancy all the time and about the cruel choice I had to make. All of a sudden life had become very serious, more serious than it should have been for a nineteen-year-old university student.

There were some unmarried women at that time who kept their children and managed somehow, but they were few and far between. I believe that those who did were actually hoping that the father of their child would change his mind and marry them once the child was born, or at least provide financial support. Perhaps they were in love with their children's fathers and therefore also loved their children. I did not have that luxury. Very few parents of unmarried mothers were willing to support them and their children. My mother told me that I could keep my baby and live with my parents. I asked her what my father had to say about that. She refused to answer. I knew without asking what my father thought. I knew that he didn't want *me* living with them, never mind an illegitimate grandchild. This was confirmed for me some months after my child was born, when I did find myself living with my parents, briefly. My father told me then, quite unequivocally, that he did not want me there. I could imagine the "welcome" I would have received with a bastard child in tow. I could not bring myself to grovel and beg from my father. If my father had ended up providing for us, my child and I would have been under a deep and lifelong obligation to him, which would have made us both very unhappy. He would have made my life a misery with his resentment and, of course, I knew that he would have made my child's life a misery too. If he had found himself supporting my child and me indefinitely, he would never have let me forget it. Throughout my childhood, my father had convinced me that I was worthless. The fact that I was pregnant seemed to prove that he had been right. I couldn't let him treat my child the same way.

People said that I could have other children, as if that would make up for it. They said that I could put it behind me and meet a nice boy and be married and make a fresh start. The implication was that no one would want to marry me if I kept the baby, but that someone might if I gave him up.

At that time, to my knowledge, there was no regular government payment to unmarried mothers. I had been raised under the good, old, Protestant work ethic, that if you had a child, you had to support your child. There was very little in the way of childcare in the late 1960s. There was no demand for childcare as very few mothers of children under school age were in the work force. The childcare that was available was clinical and uncaring and was only provided for children who were considered "at risk". Children in childcare were seen as disadvantaged and abandoned. Childcare workers did not have the time to show affection. Babies were left in cots all day and fed "by-the-clock", by whoever was on duty at the time. There were no cuddles, no kind words. I was told by professionals that children in childcare who spent their days with strangers did not bond and so would probably grow up to be psychotic at worst, delinquent at best. I was told that it would be cruel of me to keep my child and then force him to endure the daily horrors of childcare. Others convinced me that keeping my child would be selfish, that I had to put his interests first. At that time, there was no question that being at home with a full-time mother was the ideal situation for a young child. I thought that allowing him to be adopted would protect him from growing up with the stigma of illegitimacy. I didn't realise at the time that he would grow up with the stigma of being adopted instead.

Chapter 6 ... in which Evelyn waits

Having made this decision, that adoption would be best for my child, I endured the remainder of my pregnancy with a combination of resignation and fear. I deliberately suppressed any emotions that I may have developed as my child grew inside me as I was afraid of how difficult it was going to be to do finally what I felt had to be done. I tried to shut down my feelings and carry on with my life as if there were nothing unusual. I studied; I walked back and forward to lectures and climbed our stairs daily. I still socialised, went to parties, as if there were nothing out of the ordinary. Looking back, I have no idea how I would have coped without Marie. She understood me and cared for me and never let me down. I will be forever grateful to her for her unfailing support and sympathy. She remains a dear and valued friend, after all these years.

I visited my paternal grandmother (my last remaining grandparent) just before Christmas. I was very fond of her and visited her as often as I could. I felt very guilty not telling her that I was carrying her great-grandchild. She was eighty-seven years old and I thought that it would upset her and so it was easier to keep quiet about it. I was very concerned that I wouldn't be able to visit her again until after I had had the baby, as I knew I couldn't conceal my pregnancy much longer. I was worried that if I didn't see her for a long time she would think that I didn't care about her. As it happened, she died two months later. My aunt wrote me a letter, which said, "We buried your Gran last Friday." I was devastated that no one had told me in time for me to attend the funeral

At that time, student grants were paid three times per year, in a lump sum at the beginning of each term. This made it very difficult to budget. Christmas was approaching and not only was I pregnant, but it was also going to be the first Christmas I had ever spent without my family, as they were all overseas. My money was running very low and the next grant was not due until January. I wrote to my sister and asked if she could lend me some money until then. She refused. It looked like being a very miserable, lonely Christmas. Fortunately, Marie's parents kindly welcomed me into their home for Christmas, although they didn't know about my pregnancy. I spent the whole time I was there hiding my rounded tummy. Marie and I tried not to smile when her mother said that she thought I was looking thinner. Marie's friends teased me about my expanding girth with the words of a popular song, "... you're gonna carry that weight, carry that weight a long time." Little did we know for how long I was going to carry the "weight" of that pregnancy. Later in the pregnancy, Marie's father visited her sister's house unexpectedly when we were there. I was given a newspaper to hold in front of me and told that everything would be fine as long as I didn't stand up. He must have thought me very rude when everyone else walked out to the car to see him off and I sat inside "reading" the newspaper.

I contracted chickenpox while I was pregnant, which was rather embarrassing at the age of twenty. I also had a very bad bout of gastro-enteritis. I didn't eat for two weeks. Marie tried to feed me coddled eggs. I had three doctors who attended me at home, but they all said that there was nothing they could do. The third doctor who came felt my abdomen and then asked me if my periods were regular. I told her that I was five months pregnant. Perhaps she thought that I hadn't noticed.

As the pregnancy progressed, it was difficult to find suitable clothing. I had no money to invest in a maternity wardrobe and it seemed easier to conceal the pregnancy from as many people as possible, to avoid having to answer upsetting questions. Someone kindly gave me a large piece of blue material. From this, I made myself a large pinafore. I sewed every seam by hand, trimming the neckline with bias binding. Marie made me a beautiful grey cape, which I wore all through the cold Edinburgh winter. It was a severe winter, with lots of snow and ice. I was afraid often of slipping and falling, for fear it would hurt the baby. I remember walking slowly along side streets, holding on to garden fences, hand over hand. I felt particularly lonely at times like that, with no one to share the responsibility.

A few memories of my pregnancy stand out. I was very hurt on one occasion when my local church leader, to whom I had confided my news first of all, called out to me, quite casually, across the church corridor full of people, "By the way, Evelyn, the couple who are going to adopt your baby are wondering if there's any chance the baby could be coloured?" A hush fell as the implications of their question and the assumptions behind it sank in and everyone awaited my answer.

I also remember standing in a queue in Woolworth's on Princes Street one day and beginning to faint. The shop was spinning around me and my vision was blurred. I didn't know what to do. I left the queue and staggered outside for some fresh air. I sat on the pavement leaning against the wall of the shop. No one stopped to ask if I needed help. I waited there until I felt I could stand again and walked to the home of a friend in the Royal Mile. He was quite alarmed and didn't know how to help. I just needed to sit there for a while and feel safe. I also have a vivid memory of being in the Cafe Royal with a good friend when I was about seven months pregnant. He asked me about my plans for the future. I told him that the baby was to be adopted and I wept. He asked me why I was so sad about the idea of giving up my child. I told him that my biggest fear was that my child would hate me for giving him away. He then told me that he was adopted and that being adopted was fine. He didn't hate his natural mother because she gave him away, he understood that she did what she thought was best for him (many years later, thankfully, he was able to tell her that in person). That cheered me somewhat. I felt that he had turned out to be a really nice person and so maybe being adopted wasn't so bad after all.

I tried to prepare myself to deliver *their* child. In fact I had no idea how to prepare myself. Nothing in my previous experience had equipped me to deal with this situation. I had no medical preparation at all, as unmarried women were not allowed to attend antenatal classes. (When I had to attend the hospital for check-ups they always called my name out as Mrs Burns, which felt very strange because "Mrs Burns" was my mother, not me.). My doctor continued to treat me with contempt and so I did not have the confidence to ask him any questions about the forthcoming event. I had no knowledge of the mechanics of childbirth, except that it would be painful. I do not recall showing my true feelings to anyone throughout my pregnancy. I believe that I was afraid to actually allow any feelings to surface for fear that they would overwhelm me. Looking back I see myself like an emotional jack-in-the-box, with the lid held down tightly. If the lid were ever allowed to be lifted, an explosion would occur with unpredictable consequences. In spite of the support of some close friends, I felt totally isolated in my experience. I remember often lying in bed at night, alone, weeping, with the loneliness and enormity of it all. I suppose my mourning had already begun, even before my child was born. I was mourning my lost innocence, my lost lover, my lost hopes and dreams, as well as the future loss of my child. Even then, I worried about the effect on my unborn child of my deep sorrow.

The last vivid memory I have before I went into labour was of an incident that occurred three weeks before my child was born. I had sneaked into Mothercare, a large store in Princes Street which sold baby and child products. I felt as if I had no right to be there, because I wasn't a genuine expectant mother as I wasn't wearing a wedding ring. I kept my left hand in my pocket so that no one would notice. I felt as if I were not a legitimate mother-to-be, because I actually was not going to be a mother after the baby was born and I felt that if anyone found me out they would ask me to leave. I realise that these feelings may seem quite illogical, but pregnancy is not a time for logical thinking; it's a time of deep emotions. These feelings were also connected to the feeling that it was not my baby I was carrying. In spite of this, as the time to give birth drew closer, I fantasised about actually being able to care for my child, about buying nappies and bibs, like other expectant mothers. I left Mothercare, feeling very dejected and was waiting at a bus stop in Princes Street, when I met a friend. He asked me where I was going and chided me for taking the bus. He persuaded me to walk with him up the Mound (a steep hill in the centre of Edinburgh). It was a sunny, spring day in April and he was cheerful and energetic. At the top of the Mound I was breathless but persevering. I mentioned something about the upcoming birth and discovered that he didn't know that I was pregnant. I believe that he was the only person who ever congratulated me on hearing that I was pregnant. At the time I contradicted him. Now I bless him. At the time I couldn't see anything to be happy about; the whole business seemed to me to be destined to end in misery. This warm, generous man told me that whenever a child comes into the world, there is joy. I think that that was my first clue that I could love my child. But by that stage I had convinced myself that I had to follow through with my logical, sensible plan and that emotions couldn't be allowed to sway me. Looking back, the biggest mistake I made was thinking that I had to make a decision early in my pregnancy. Because I allowed the church to arrange the adoption then, I felt obligated to go through with the plan and not let everyone down. Because I felt committed to the adoption, I deliberately suppressed my feelings for my child and didn't allow an emotional relationship with him to develop. I should have waited and allowed nature to take its course. If I had, I would have been more in tune with my feelings after my son was born and I would have known that I could love him.

My mother decided to come to Scotland for the birth. I remember going to the airport to meet her. I hadn't seen her for nearly a year. I only ever saw my mother cry twice in her life. The first time was when her own mother died. The second was when she saw me in an advanced state of pregnancy, at Edinburgh airport. Mum stayed in the flat with us for a couple of weeks. We

41

had dreadful beds, which sagged terribly. Mum was so small and so slight that when she lay in the bed you didn't even know she was there, the covers lay so flat.

My baby was due on the 15th of May. I knew that the baby would come very close to that date because I knew exactly when he was conceived (looking back, I think he may have been conceived on the weekend that the Woodstock Festival took place, but I wasn't feeling particularly full of peace, love and music at the time). In fact, he was born at 13.13 on Saturday 16th May 1970. On the afternoon of Friday May 15th, I was in the university lecture theatre watching a Rolling Stones film. I felt pains in my stomach and started to watch the clock. I turned to Marie and said that I was having pains every fifteen minutes. She asked did I want to go home. No fear, I wanted to see the end of the film. We went home afterwards and timed my pains for several more hours. There was not a lot of progress but the pains continued. At 11.45 pm we rang for a taxi and my mother accompanied me to the hospital. I was separated from her as soon as we entered the hospital. The rule was that only husbands were allowed in the maternity unit. If you didn't have a husband, too bad, you were not allowed a substitute. My mother sat in the waiting room until 6.00 am but they refused to let her see me. It was a large hospital and she had no idea where to find me. I was bathed (I had to kneel, not sit) and put in a bed in a dark room with the curtains round my bed. There was no nurse in the room and no doctor visited me.

There were other beds, which held other women, in various stages of labour. During the night some of them were taken out, screaming and crying in pain. I had no way of summoning assistance. At one point during the night I needed to go to the toilet and I called out several times. There was no one there; no one heard me. I got out of bed and tried to find the toilet, but couldn't. No one visited me, no one spoke to me, no one checked to see if I were all right. I was terrified.

I lay awake all night and then found myself next morning in the delivery room. My mother, by this time, had given up and gone home. Strangely, I have no memory of pain during the birth itself. I have no idea if I was drugged as the hospital refused to allow me access to my medical records when I requested them years later. My labour seemed to be very slow and I believe that I was given something to hurry things along. I remember being asked whether or not I had practised my breathing exercises. To explain why I didn't know anything about breathing exercises all I had to say was, "I'm not married." That explained everything. Everyone knew that if you weren't married you weren't allowed to go to antenatal classes. Rules were rules.

Chapter 7 ... in which Evelyn's baby is born

Giving birth was an event in which I didn't feel that I took part. I believe that's why I can't remember the pain. I detached myself from the experience. It seemed that childbirth happened not to me, but in spite of me. I remember that there was a moment of panic, that there were calls for a doctor. I was afraid - of course I was afraid. I had no idea what was happening and the medical staff seemed to take charge of everything and deliberately exclude me from the proceedings. I have no idea whether they treated me that way because I was unmarried or if they treated every woman like that. The doctor arrived and the baby was delivered with the help of forceps. I discovered afterwards that he had become stuck in the birth canal. I learned that if I had gone into labour when I was alone (as some young, frightened women still do) and had not obtained medical assistance, the baby and I would both have died; the child first and then me. Anecdotal evidence suggests that birth difficulties are common in cases where babies are to be adopted. It's as if the mothers somehow try to hold on to them for as long as possible.

Someone told me that I had a son. I was surprised. I was surprised that I had a baby at all. In spite of having had nine months to get used to the idea, I still found it hard to believe that all this was really happening to me. The midwife handed my baby to me when he was born and I held him. I don't know if that was done deliberately or if they didn't realise that he was to be adopted, but I will be forever grateful that it happened. We gazed at each other for a few moments, my little man and I. When I looked at him, my immediate feeling was one of enormous pride. I was amazed that I had produced this living thing; that this brand new little person had come out of me. I realised there and then, in that split second when I saw him and held him, that he was a whole new person who had nothing to do with betrayal, rape or anger. He was fresh, new and mine. Looking back I realise that, at that moment, I knew that I could love him after all. But it was too late, too late to change my mind. His prospective adoptive parents were anxiously awaiting him. I had promised them my child and I couldn't go back on my word. Hadn't I thought it all out and hadn't I realised that it was for the best? Just seeing him didn't change any of that, didn't change the facts - the facts that I had no job, no husband, no money and not even a decent place to stay. I felt that I had nothing to offer him except my love, but I couldn't see how love could feed and clothe him. Yes, I did love him then, but I felt that it would be selfish of me to keep him.

After the birth my son was taken from me and put into the hospital nursery. I was placed in a large ward with about forty beds, each with a new mother and each with a new baby beside the bed, twenty-four hours a day. That was the hospital policy. There was a baby by every bed except mine, that is. All day and all night I heard babies crying, watched mothers tend to them, hold them, kiss them and feed them. I wasn't even allowed to draw the curtains around my bed and be alone with my pain, except at rest time in the afternoons. Every day I watched happy husbands and grandparents visit all those other mothers, bringing them flowers and gifts, cooing and laughing and discussing whom the new babies looked like. I remember one friend did bring me flowers to the hospital. I was angry with her, although I realise now that she meant well. I felt that flowers were for celebration. For me, this was a tragedy. I didn't feel that flowers were appropriate and she seemed not to understand that. For those other mothers there were lots of hugs and kisses, lots of smiles. It seemed such a cruel punishment to have to watch everyone else's joy when I was suffering so much. If they noticed that I didn't have a baby with me, they whispered and looked disapproving. Some of them looked as if they felt sorry for me. I certainly felt very sorry for myself. Every night I spent in the hospital I cried myself to sleep and had awful nightmares. When my milk started to come in I was very surprised. I hadn't been warned that this would happen. I thought you only made milk if you started to breast-feed. My breasts were bound tightly. It was very painful.

And I felt so very sorry for my son, because he wasn't being welcomed into the world the way all those other babies were and that reminded me that I didn't feel accepted as a child and now I didn't feel accepted as a mother. I trusted the people who were going to adopt him to welcome him, to give him the hugs and kisses that he wasn't getting in the hospital. I trusted them to give him the unconditional love and acceptance that I never got from my father. Looking back, I realise how naive I was to assume that because a child was adopted, all this would necessarily follow.

The social worker at the hospital had told me that I had to give my son a name. I had mixed feelings about that. It seemed pointless, as I knew that his name would be changed when he was adopted. It felt like a token admission by the authorities that I was really his mother. I thought that it was an empty gesture on their part to acknowledge me as his mother briefly, but then take my motherhood from me for the rest of my life. They told me to forget about him and "get on with my life". I only discovered many years later that it's not forgetting your lost child that allows you to get on with your life, but remembering him.

I had mixed feelings about spending time with my baby. Mum and Marie asked if they could go to the nursery to see him. They told me that he was beautiful. Mum said that his ears were like my father's. In one way I wanted to see him. I was very drawn to him and desperately wanted to hold him, but I was afraid of how painful it would be. I thought that the more time I spent with him the harder it would be to part with him and at this stage in the proceedings, I didn't think that I had any choice but to do just that.

A few days after the birth, however, I knew that I wanted to see my son, no matter what. I didn't ask permission; I was afraid that they would refuse. I frantically wandered the corridors until I found the nursery. I asked the nurse if I could look at him. She was very kind and said that I could hold him if I wanted to and told me about his feeds and his progress. I sat with him in my arms for a little while. I looked at his tiny fingers and unwrapped him to see his tiny toes. I pressed my face against his ever-so-soft cheek and kissed his smooth forehead. I whispered in his little ear, "I love you. I will always love you and you will always be welcome in my life." Then the doctor arrived with a group of students. He was very angry that I had been allowed to see my son and shouted at the nurse and at me, very rudely. He told me that if I "didn't want him" I should just "leave him alone". He was scornful and hurtful and I could see the students lower their heads with embarrassment. I wanted to kick him and shout back at him, but I felt so powerless. I held on to my baby until he had left the room, however and only then did I creep back to bed. I wasn't going to let him think that he only had to speak for me to obey. Although I was pathetically compliant throughout the whole process, I had still a little spark of rebellion left in me. He gave orders that no one was to see my baby after that and when my mother tried to see him again the next day, she was turned away. For years afterwards I used to mutter darkly whenever I thought of that doctor, "He'll be the first to go when the revolution comes."

Chapter 8 ... in which Evelyn's baby is taken away

When my son was six days old I was told that my church leader, who had arranged the adoption and his wife were coming to collect him from the hospital the following day. The next day came and I cried and sobbed for hours. I can still hear myself saying over and over, "They're taking him away today, they're taking him away today." Finally the doctor decided to sedate me. I think that I was disturbing the other mothers. I should have known, and they should have known, that when I became hysterical, that meant that I really didn't want to give him up. It seems obvious now but at the time no one thought that way. No one seemed to think that I needed help, just sedation. No one said to themselves, "This young woman is obviously very upset at the thought of losing her child, maybe she should reconsider." All those professional people, doctors, nurses, social workers and they didn't consider what my hysteria meant. They could only think of controlling it, not exploring or understanding it.

I waited for the couple who were collecting my son to come to speak to me, to offer me some words of comfort, perhaps reassure me that I was doing what was best for my child, that he would go to a good home. No one came near. I waited and waited and finally I decided that I would try to see my son one more time, to say goodbye, before they took him from me. I went back to the nursery and looked around. My baby was gone. They had taken him without even telling me. I felt that I must be beneath their contempt, that they couldn't lower themselves to visit me. I also felt that I was totally insignificant, that they only wanted my child, but didn't want to become involved with me as a person, or my feelings. I wanted to be acknowledged as my son's mother. After all, I was still legally his mother at that time. Perhaps they were afraid that if they talked to me about the adoption, I might change my mind. It seemed that my child had to be taken surreptitiously, that it couldn't be done openly. It was as if everyone was conspiring to pretend that it wasn't happening. Whatever the reason, I felt very hurt and insulted. No one from the church ever mentioned my child again.

Once my son was gone I desperately wanted to get out of the hospital. I kept asking when could I go home. The doctor visited me the following day and told me that as I had developed a post-natal uterine infection, I would have to stay in hospital for a few more days. I had what used to be called "childbed fever". Left untreated, it can be fatal. I told him that I couldn't stay any longer as my final exams started the next day. He told me that I could go home that day, but that I would be putting my health at risk. I didn't care about my health. It was of no importance to me. I just wanted to get out of there. I hadn't lied, my exams did start the following day.

I remember leaving the hospital. It was as if I was looking at the world through glass, as if I was not really present and not really interacting. I felt detached from my physical body and quite drained of any emotion. Two days after I was released from hospital, my mother and I went to the Registry Office in George Square to register the birth. I had decided to call my son Adam, as it seemed an appropriate name for a first-born. His middle name was George, after my brother, as he was born on my brother's birthday. At the Registry Office I was asked, "Are you married to your baby's father?", then, "Is the baby's father here to have his name recorded on the birth certificate?", then, "Are you keeping your baby or is he to be adopted?" After answering all of those embarrassing questions in a very public place, I watched as the word "Adopted" was written carefully on the bottom of his birth certificate. Even then, I remember thinking that it hadn't actually happened yet and how dare they do that. Because it was a private adoption, I also had to answer very personal questions at a later stage. I was horrified to be asked whether or not any money had changed hands. I felt guilty enough that I had given my baby away and now they wanted to know if I had sold him.

The day after I left the hospital I was at the university for an exam. I went into the cafeteria and one of the women working there noticed that I had obviously had my baby.

"What did you have?" she cooed.

"A boy."

"And did you manage to get him into child care?"

"Yes."

There began the lies. Already I was denying my experience. I couldn't bring myself to try to explain to her what had really happened. I knew that I would never see her again and so I would not have to keep up the pretence. I never set foot in the cafeteria again. I wanted to be away from the university, away from Edinburgh. I needed to escape, but I couldn't leave until my exams were over.

The next few weeks passed in a blur. Mum left and everyone else went on with their lives as if it was all over. I sat my final exams. I felt numb and empty. I felt drained of all feeling. I was wounded to the very depths of my being. I felt as if my life were over. I spent a lot of time in Greyfriars Churchyard, among the dead. I felt dead inside and wished that I were lying among them.

In the early stages of my pregnancy, I had met a young man called Tony and had gone out with him for a while. I told him that I was pregnant and that I was planning to give the baby up for adoption. When I was about five months pregnant, he set off to travel across Asia and Europe. He sent me bright postcards from Delhi, Kabul, Istanbul and other exotic places as I struggled through the last months of my pregnancy. Finally, just after my exams had finished, I got a letter from him saying that his next stop would be Athens. I had no idea at that time what to do with myself. I had no job and couldn't even begin to think of looking for one. I stayed home a lot as I dreaded meeting people who might ask about the baby. I was feeling quite disconnected and so I decided, on the spur of the moment, to go and meet him in Athens. I wrote him a letter to the American Express office asking him to meet me off the train and bought a one-way ticket. I had no idea what I was going to do when I arrived in Athens, nor how I was going to get home, but I didn't care. I felt reckless. I felt that nothing mattered anyway. After what I had been through, these were very small matters, of little importance. My doctor was opposed to the idea and stressed the importance of my six-week check-up. I had been very attentive to medical matters when I was pregnant, but that was only because I cared what happened to my baby. I didn't care what happened to me. It was a matter of sheer indifference to me whether I was healthy or not.

On the Acropolis Express (yes, that was actually its name), I met Laurie, a delightful social worker from New York, and we became firm friends. Laurie was going to be married soon and her fiancé had agreed to her fulfilling her dream to tour Europe before the wedding. The Acropolis Express took us all the way across Europe, through Frankfurt and Belgrade, and finally, after a journey of three days, to Athens. We arrived in Athens in the evening. There was no one there to meet me. My heart sank. Laurie was wonderful and kept my spirits up. We set off in search of a youth hostel. The hostel was exciting, full of young people from around the world, each with an interesting story to tell. I pretended that I was just like them, young and single, with no responsibilities. I didn't dare tell anyone that I had just had a child. It was a relief to me to be among strangers who didn't know anything about me - and so the lies continued.

The next day Laurie and I went to the American Express office. My letter had been collected. I couldn't understand why Tony wasn't there to meet me if he had received my letter. I had no idea what to do next and very little money. Laurie persuaded me to forget about my worries and join her on a tourist walk around the city. We climbed Likavitos Hill and afterwards accidentally wandered into the grounds of the royal palace, where we were confronted by armed guards. The sun shone and the city appeared to me to be exotic and exciting. In the evening we took in the Son et Lumière show at the Acropolis. I wore a summer T-shirt dress. Laurie told me that I looked very nice except that I needed to do something about my stomach. She had no idea that it was only three weeks since I had left the hospital, after giving birth. It was wonderful to be away from the place where I had suffered so much, but I was concerned about where I was going to go from there. I spent another night in the youth hostel. I had so little money, I asked if I could sleep on the balcony, which was cheaper than a bunk, but I was told that women were not allowed to sleep on the balcony. Next morning I came down for breakfast and there was Tony in the hallway. He had actually spent the night in the same hostel. Over breakfast I heard his story.

He had arrived in Athens and gone to the American Express office to see if there was any mail from me but it was closed for the afternoon siesta. He had very little money left and so he went from there to the British Consulate to see if they could help him to get home. They arranged for him to work his passage back on a boat and he signed up, giving them his passport (which was necessary in order to book his place). He then returned to American Express, got my letter saying that I was arriving the next day, tried in vain to get out of the boat arrangement and had to leave that night. When the boat docked in Piraeus, he travelled back up to Athens to look for me. He discovered that there were three youth hostels in Athens and decided that he would try each one in turn. He had only one night and one day to get back to the boat. Amazingly, he went first of all to the hostel that I was staying in. He had arrived there late at night and they said that it was too late for him to check if I was there and so he spent the night and I found him there in the morning. If he had gone to another hostel first, I could have been anywhere by the time he had reached my hostel and we might never have met up at all. We spent the day together and then he had to travel back to Piraeus to rejoin his boat.

After seeing him off on the train, I went back to the hostel and decided to have a look on the notice board to see if I could get a lift somewhere in the direction of home. As I was looking, a young man approached with a sign to pin up. Before he did, he said to those standing around the board, "Anyone want a lift to London?" I couldn't believe my luck. He was with two friends. They were final year law students from the south of England. There were supposed to be four of them on the holiday, but the other friend had found out that his girlfriend was pregnant and cancelled at the last minute. I sold some blood at the local hospital in order to be able to contribute some money for petrol. This journey became a real adventure for me, which distracted me for a while from my sorrow. I set off with them and we spent some time on a little island called Skiathos, sleeping and eating on the beach. That time was actually very relaxing for me. It was an escape. We walked three miles into the village every day to buy fresh fruit and vegetables from the market and drank water from the spring. On the beach I met an American girl who was travelling and reading *Catch 22*. To keep her backpack as light as possible, she ripped out and threw away each chapter of the book as she read it. I was horrified that someone would defile a book like that. However, I retrieved her discarded chapters and began to read the book, albeit from the middle. I had spent so much time crying and so little time laughing in recent months that I thought that I had forgotten how, but *Catch 22* made me laugh out loud. It remains one of my favourite books. I was wishing that I could stay there forever and escape from what felt to me like a very cruel world. All the way across Europe we met other travellers. It was a time of escape and adventure for many young people and travelling was a relatively safe activity at that time. We moved on through Salonika, to Sarajevo, an ancient and rather forbidding city. I am so glad that I got to see it before it was so badly damaged in later years. We were travelling in a rather unreliable landrover but it took us, over the next few weeks, all the way along the Dalmatian Coast, which was spectacular, across to Venice, where I was forbidden to enter the Doge's Palace because my arms were bare, over the San Bernadino pass where we encountered an avalanche and then descended almost immediately (so it seemed) into a bright summer day in the valley, into Switzerland and finally, through Cologne, where the cathedral was under repair, back to Ostende. Being in other countries, with people who knew nothing about me except what I chose to tell them, soothed me somewhat. I was becoming adept at concealment. At Ostende there was a letter waiting for me from Marie to tell me that I had passed my final exams. Although I had managed to pass my exams, I couldn't bring myself to attend my graduation ceremony. I couldn't face all those smiling, confident students, optimistic about the future. Besides, no one from my family was going to be there in the audience to applaud me. I have completed two post-graduate courses since then, but I still cannot face a graduation ceremony.

I arrived back in Edinburgh before Tony did, much to his surprise. I was very restless and unhappy. I had no idea what I wanted to do or where I wanted to be. I was drifting, mentally and physically and I think I would have gone anywhere with anyone. Tony was keen to go to Bermuda, as he had never been there. I wrote to my mother and she lent me some money and we planned to set off. Before leaving Edinburgh, however, I had to sign the consent form for my son to be adopted. I have only a vague memory of this event. In my mind and in my heart he already did not belong to me and so the actual signing of the form was almost a technicality. I left Edinburgh, with Tony, in September 1970 and have never lived there since then.

First of all we went to Brussels and then Amsterdam and Luxembourg. In Brussels we stayed at the youth hostel, with a host of hopeful illegal immigrants, desperate to buy passports to enter the United Kingdom. We walked all over the city, buying apple waffles in the Grande Place. It rained every day. In Amsterdam we lived on a barge, learned how to use the trams and mixed with the international bevy of young people that descended on the city in the 1960s and 1970s. I bought *Bound for Glory*, Woody Guthrie's autobiography. I still have it. When we got to Luxembourg airport it was covered with flags. We witnessed the arrival of President Tito as we awaited our flight to New York. I didn't really care where we went. I was totally aimless and hopeless at the same time. Before we boarded the aeroplane, we were taken aside and searched. I think they thought that Tony was a terrorist because he was of mixed race. We set off for New

York. We travelled by Icelandic Airways, because it was the cheapest of all, via Iceland. We stopped in Reykjavik, where, looking out of the aeroplane, the sea looked frozen and the landscape looked Martian. When we walked into the airport terminal, we thought our extremities would drop off from the cold. When everyone reboarded the aeroplane after the stopover in Reykjavik, there were several people wandering up and down the aisles, looking lost and confused. The captain announced that they had accidentally overbooked and would six people like to volunteer to spend the night in a luxury hotel in Reykjavik, courtesy of the airline. As the aeroplane was full of itinerant young people, many of whom had not slept in a real bed for months, there was a rush of volunteers.

We travelled on to New York and stayed a few days with Laurie. Then we parted company. I travelled on to Bermuda and he was supposed to follow me, but he never did. I should have expected that, I suppose, given my track record with men. I never heard from him again. I set off from Laurie's apartment in Brooklyn (on her wedding day) at about 6.00 am with five dollars to try to find my way to Kennedy Airport, to catch the flight to Bermuda. By the time I actually arrived at the airport, after various bus and train rides, I was down to my last dollar. I collected my rucksack from the left luggage and set off for the appropriate terminal. The bag was heavy and so I decided to get a taxi. I could see where I was going; it wasn't far. I was sure a dollar would cover the fare. What I didn't know was that traffic only went one way at Kennedy Airport and so the taxi set off in the opposite direction from what I had expected. All I could do was watch the meter and when it came to a dollar I would have to stop the cab and get out. At ninety-five cents, we reached my terminal. I went to check in and they told me that my flight was boarding at 10.00 am. I looked at the clock. It was 9.59 am. I went to the appropriate gate and there was a queue of people there. I realised as I got near the front of the queue that they were handing over money. When it came my turn I was asked for $3.00 departure tax.

I said, "I only have five cents."

The young woman was very polite. "What currency do you have?"

"None."

"Is it travellers' cheques that you have?"

"No, I don't have any of those either. I have no money."

"You're travelling to Bermuda and you have no money?"

"That's right."

She called the manager. He politely went through all the same possibilities before he finally understood that all I had was five cents. I offered to post the three dollars to him after I arrived in Bermuda. By this time all the other passengers were seated on a bus, waiting to go across the tarmac to our plane, staring at me malevolently for holding them up. Finally they let me go on the plane.

Chapter 9 ... in which Evelyn moves to Bermuda

When I arrived in Bermuda I decided that I would call my mother, but it cost ten cents for a telephone call and I only had five. Then, amazingly, I spotted my sister. She had come to the airport to witness the arrival of the first-ever jumbo jet to land in Bermuda and to her surprise, I stepped off it. I hadn't even noticed that the plane that I was on was in any way different from other aeroplanes that I had travelled on. I arrived in Bermuda with five cents and a few clothes to my name. I kept that five cents and later had it made into a ring to remind me of my experience.

My parents were living in a tiny, one-bedroomed flat attached to a home of which my mother was housekeeper. They had no room for me and it wasn't my home, but I had no home, no money and no idea where else to go. My mother made me welcome, of course. My father said, bluntly, "I don't want you here." I was determined to find a job and move into a flat as soon as I could. I had been desperate to get out of Edinburgh, where my child was born, to escape from the memories and now I found myself back in Bermuda, where he had been conceived. I made enquiries and found out that the father of my child had left Bermuda just after I did. I was relieved that I did not have to face him. Those early weeks in Bermuda were very difficult. On the one hand it was a kind of fresh start and good for me to be away from where I had been so miserable, but, on the other hand, I knew no one except my immediate family members and I was very lonely. I didn't want to be there, but then I didn't really want to be anywhere at that particular time. I had no work experience to speak of and, although I had a degree, I wasn't actually qualified to do anything. I contacted the Department of Education and asked about teaching positions. I tried for other jobs too, but to no avail. Then one Friday I was sunbathing in my bikini when I got a call from the headmaster of the Berkeley Institute.

He said, "I believe you're looking for a teaching position here in Bermuda?"

"Yes."

"Can you start on Monday?"

It's the only job interview I ever did dressed in a bikini. When I arrived at the school, I discovered that the reason that they needed me immediately was because the teacher I was replacing had had a nervous breakdown, after only two months at the school. Learning to be a teacher on-the-job was hard work and there were times when I wanted to give it up, but I had no money to go anywhere else and so I stuck it out. I spent six weeks with my parents. It was a very sad and lonely time, especially having to endure my father's constant disapproval. Once I secured a job, I moved out and found a flat. My plan was to pay Mum back the money that I had borrowed and then leave. I had no idea where I would go, but I didn't feel at all welcome or at home in Bermuda. Shortly after arriving there, I had my twenty-first birthday. It was a rather dismal affair. The only people who were there were my sister and my parents, because they were the only people that I knew in Bermuda. My mother felt that after having some birthday cake, we should all go out somewhere. My sister and my father refused. Mum and I went to a night-club, to mark the occasion. There was a professional photographer there, going around the tables taking photographs. Mum suddenly remembered that she had left her false teeth behind and couldn't smile for the photograph. As it happened, his camera broke down just before he reached our table. It felt fitting to me. I had the odd sensation that I wasn't quite real and that if I had had a photograph taken, I would not have appeared in it.

Within six months I had paid Mum back the money that I had borrowed from her, but I decided that I should stay until the end of the school year, as I didn't want to let the school down. By the end of my first year there I was thoroughly enjoying the work and starting to feel more at home. After four years there I loved Bermuda, the school, the staff and the students and it was a great wrench to leave.

In Bermuda, for the first time in my life, I lived alone. I wondered why I hadn't thought of it sooner. I loved living alone. I did make friends in Bermuda and many of them are still friends to this day. None of them knew about my son, of course. My deception continued and became more entrenched. The more time passes, the more deeply buried the secret becomes and the harder it is to think of revealing it. While I was living in Bermuda, I made lots of visits to New York, to Boston and back to Scotland. In New York I wandered Greenwich Village, soaking up the atmosphere, buying books and jewellery. On one trip I paid a taxi driver to drive me from one end of McDougall Street to the other so that I could say that I had driven past Bob Dylan's house. I had no idea which one it was and so I drove past all of them just to be sure. I risked my life in the West Village to buy the cheapest-ever Afghan coat, which I wore for many years to come. I think it was the only one Renfrew had ever seen. In Boston I walked through the grounds of Harvard University, just so that I could say, "I went through Harvard (in the front gate and out the back)."

During this time I took up yoga, which I found very beneficial. I have often drawn on the techniques that I learned in yoga throughout my life and have found them very useful. In one class we performed a meditation in which we were required to focus on an apple. We closed our eyes, relaxed and imagined our apple, its smell, its colour and its texture. We took our apple on a trip from when it grew on the tree to when it came into our possession. I was amazed at how my meditation took on a life of its own, seemingly outwith my control. My apple was beautiful, healthy, shiny and colourful as it grew on the tree. Eventually I bought it, in a paper bag, from a fruit shop. As I walked down the street I thought about eating my apple and looked forward to the pleasure it would give me. I drew it from the bag and held it in front of my face to admire it for a moment first. All I could see was a large, ugly bruise. My apple was damaged. It didn't take much for me to work out that that was how I felt about myself. I might appear at first glance to be attractive and desirable, but on closer inspection I would be found to be ugly and unappetising. For many years I worked very hard not to let anyone get close enough to find out. Many years later I discovered that not only did many natural mothers feel this way about themselves, but that many adopted people also saw themselves as somehow damaged and second-rate.

Not long after the loss of my son I began to have frightening dreams, nightmares perhaps. They were of two types, dreams of exposure and dreams of separation. In the dreams of exposure I would find myself having a shower or sitting on the toilet when all of a sudden I would realise that I was in the middle of a department store or on a busy street, with everyone looking at me. I would panic and feel very exposed and want to hide myself. In the dreams of separation I would be perhaps on a bus or a train with a baby and then I would get off without thinking and leave the baby behind. As I watched the vehicle speed off into the distance with my baby, I would realise, too late, that I had been careless and had let my baby go. I felt guilty and worthless. Many other natural mothers have since talked to me about their dreams. Often they dream about hearing a baby crying and trying desperately, in vain, to locate it. My dreams haunted me for many years.

While I was in Bermuda I thought of my child every day. I looked at other babies and wondered if he was sitting up yet, if he was walking, talking, what he looked like. I carried the picture of his little face with me in my mind and held on to it tenaciously. It was the one thing that no one could take from me. I also took up a voluntary position, teaching young women who had left school early because of a pregnancy. As I worked with these young women, I envied them so much because they were raising their children. I wanted to do all that I could to support them. I also was instrumental in persuading my headmaster to change the school policy on young, pregnant women having to leave school. Not that the school had a written policy, as such, but whenever a student announced that she was pregnant, the assumption was that she would leave school as soon as possible. One of my most promising students became pregnant at the age of thirteen. I met with her and her mother and encouraged her to stay on at school as long as possible. She was extremely brave and continued with her studies. The headmaster called me into his office and asked wasn't it about time she should be leaving school. I told him that I saw no reason why she should leave; she was in perfectly good health and an excellent student. I persuaded him to see the logic in my argument and she continued at school until a few days before her child was born. She had excellent family support and was able to complete her education and now has a beautiful home and a prominent position in the workforce. She remains a very good friend and I am privileged to be her daughter's godmother.

Having got it so wrong, ie been pregnant without being married, I really wanted to get it right. I got married, in Bermuda, three years after losing my son. I had only known my husband for about three months when we married. Just as well my Grandmother wasn't still around or she would have been muttering, "Marry in haste, repent at your leisure." I told my husband before we were married that I had had a son and he accepted that, but he never mentioned it again. My husband had also lost a child through adoption and so I felt that he would understand my pain. When I was suffering and missing my son over the years, however, I was never able to share that pain with my husband. Fortunately, we managed later to build a relationship with the daughter that he had given up for adoption and she and I still keep in touch.

We decided that we wanted to have a child as soon as possible after we were married. I became pregnant five months into the marriage. We were delighted. I thought that this time I had got it right. I had a loving husband and I was expecting a child that was planned and wanted. I happily announced my pregnancy to friends and family. When I was about three months pregnant,

61

however, I realised that my husband's behaviour had become bizarre and frightening. I don't know whether it had anything to do with the pregnancy or not. I begged him to seek professional help. He flatly refused and would not accept that there was any problem. I realised that I had made a big mistake, that I could never be happy with him, that I had misjudged yet another man. I only learned several years later that he was suffering from a serious personality disorder. Perhaps if he had agreed to address this disorder early in our marriage, things could have turned out differently.

I became very depressed, as I felt trapped. After what I had gone through in my first pregnancy I did not feel that I could leave my husband and go through another pregnancy alone. After thinking that I had got my life back on track and had made a positive move, I now felt that I had gone from one disaster to another. After having gone through the trauma of announcing my first pregnancy to everyone and having to deal with their disapproval and now having told everyone that I was pregnant again, I couldn't bring myself to announce that my marriage was over, after less than a year. I was struggling to convince myself that I wasn't a total failure in life. I decided to battle on and conceal my unhappiness. While I was pregnant, my husband decided that he wanted to live in Scotland, in spite of the fact that he had been born and raised in Bermuda and all of his family was there. In 1974, I found myself back in Renfrew again, with just a suitcase of clothes to my name, making another fresh start.

Chapter 10 ... in which Evelyn returns to Renfrew

Having my second child, the first child of my marriage, was a very confusing time for me. It was important for the hospital to know whether or not this was my first child because there were different arrangements for first time mothers. When it came to caring for a child, feeding, bathing, handling, it was my first child, but physically, of course, it was my second. Every time I was asked the question, it hurt. I couldn't pretend to medical people that I hadn't already had a child as there were physical signs that I had, but I wanted to make it clear that I knew nothing about looking after babies, because I desperately wanted to know everything there was to know about caring for a baby as I needed to be the best mother possible to this child. I was so afraid that something would go wrong. I felt that I didn't deserve to have a child and refused to look ahead to bringing my child home from hospital. I thought that someone (either a real person or Fate) would find me out, realise that I had given away a child and decide that I wasn't fit to have another one. I couldn't even bring myself to buy anything for my baby before I went into hospital, not even a nappy, in case I somehow jinxed myself. There was only one thing I had prepared for him. I had spent many hours crocheting a large, round, white shawl to wrap him in. Before he was born my husband cut it to pieces in a fit of temper. I hadn't the heart to start another.

When I was in labour, my baby's heart stopped beating. I wasn't surprised. I thought, "This is it, I knew I'd never be allowed to have this baby to keep." He survived that, only to develop jaundice. And so I found myself, yet again, the only mother in the ward without a baby by her bed, as he was in the special baby unit for several days. I was bereft. I thought everyone must know that I wasn't like other mothers. When I went to the unit to feed him, I couldn't wake him. I sat and held him and cried, convinced that he was going to die. Then they said that I could go home, but that my son would have to stay in hospital for further treatment. I became very upset and refused to go. There was no way I was going to walk out of a maternity hospital again with no baby. I thought that if I left him there I would never see him again. I have a very clear memory of actually bringing him home from the hospital. I carried him up the pathway to the house, treading carefully on the frozen, sparkling, white snow and just as I reached the door I looked over my shoulder, convinced that this was too good to be true and that someone was going to step forward and say, "Where do you think you're going with that baby?"

I faced the same dilemma with the birth of each subsequent child, when answering the question, "How many children have you had already?", but it was more poignant with the first. I read book after book on child and baby care. I felt that I had to prove myself, to prove that I was worthy to have the care of these children. I thought that if I had lots of children that I would somehow fill the empty space left by the loss of my first child. I had four children in the space of five years. They filled my time, if not the empty space left by their brother. In their early years, I devoted myself totally to my children. None of my children ever had a bottle; they were completely breast-fed. I breast-fed the first and third children of my marriage until I was five months pregnant with the second and fourth. None of my children ever ate prepared baby foods. I cooked everything for them myself. I never used disposable nappies, in spite of having two babies in nappies for a considerable period of time. No one was going to be able to say that I wasn't a good mother.

In my six years of marriage I endured every kind of domestic abuse - physical, emotional and sexual. I also had four children. All of my children were planned and wanted and I was very grateful for them. They brought me much joy. I chose to be a full time mother to them when they were very young. I left the paid workforce when I was pregnant with the first of my four children and did not return to work until the youngest was in kindergarten. I made the choice to forego material possessions in order that my children would not lack maternal love and care in their early years. I never regretted that choice. I believe that my children benefited much more from the time that I spent with them than they would have from any increase in our standard of living. The ten years that I spent out of paid employment were a wonderful investment in my children's lives. I hear parents say that they cannot afford to stay home to care for their babies. I don't know how they think that they can afford not to.

There were many good times in my marriage, but my husband was so unpredictable that I could never relax with him, even when things seemed to be going well for a while. When I was seven months pregnant with the second child of my marriage, my husband was drinking heavily. He sometimes came home drunk from work, after spending several hours in the pub and then complained that his meal wasn't ready. Sometimes he threw things. One night he came home drunk and lost his temper over nothing at all. He lifted our old birdcage stand. It was very heavy with a thick, metal base. He swung it at me. I turned my back to protect the baby and he hit me several times on my back and legs, bruising me badly. He then lifted it over his head and I just had time to think, "If he hits me on my head with that, he'll kill me", before he stopped himself. It was the first time he had ever hit me. A friend once told me that if a man hits you once, he may hit you again or he may not, but if he hits you twice he will always hit you. I decided to give him another chance, although he refused to apologise. In fact, he refused to take responsibility for his actions. He said that he was drunk and couldn't remember hitting me and so there was no need for him to apologise.

A few months later I met up with an old friend and that meeting brought home to me how unhappy I was. I had met my very first boyfriend at a New Year's party when I was sixteen. His name was Billy. His mother had died just a few weeks before and he lived alone with his father, the youngest of a large family. We were childhood sweethearts really. He lived around the corner from me and our relationship was very innocent, but very close. We used to do our homework together. My mother really liked him and felt sorry for him. She always wanted to feed him. We were boyfriend and girlfriend for about six months, although when I think of the impact Billy had on my life, I imagine that it was much longer. I believe that he was the first male ever to adore me. He was good and he was honest. We moved on, but we remained friends. We saw each other occasionally over the years, but not often. After I had been married for two and a half years and had two children, I heard that he had cancer. I was very upset and wanted to see him. I had no idea where he was living, as I hadn't seen him for several years, but I remembered where his sister lived. I decided to go to her house to find out how he was. I never forgot his birthday and I turned up on his sister's doorstep on his twenty-seventh birthday. His niece answered the door.

"You probably don't remember me, but I used to be a friend of your Uncle Billy's."

"I'll just tell him you're here."

I was astounded. He was there. "Don't tell him who it is, I want to surprise him."

Billy came downstairs and threw his arms around me and told me that seeing me was the best birthday present he could ever have had.

Yes, he had cancer, but he was hoping that the operation had been a success and that it was gone. We caught up on what had been happening in our lives and the lives of old friends and promised to see each other again. I told my husband that I had seen Billy, explained that he was just an old friend and that I visited him because he was ill. My husband was very angry and said that I was never to see Billy again. I am so glad that I disregarded what he said, although I never mentioned Billy's name to him again. I saw Billy a few times over the next nine months. Billy asked me if I were happily married. I wasn't at all. I was thoroughly miserable, but I felt that if I told Billy that, he would want to save me and protect me. I knew that he still cared for me and I had always had very warm feelings for him.

I felt that, because Billy was so ill, I didn't want him worrying about me and I didn't want him to feel that he should help me out. Billy would have been very angry if he had known how my husband had treated me. I told him that I was very happily married and had a very good husband. I was sinking deeper into more lies and more deception. He said that he was delighted to hear that because I deserved the best. I was very unhappy lying to Billy. There were already too many lies in my life. There were times when I almost told him the truth. I was desperately unhappy and afraid, but I was also afraid of Billy getting involved and so I kept up my charade, in order to protect him. Our relationship at this period of my life was purely platonic.

I was becoming more and more concerned about his health and I spent a week trying to ring him to find out how he was, but getting no reply. Finally I found out that he was at his sister's house. I rang there. His nephew, a medical student, answered the telephone. I asked to speak to Billy. He was too weak to come to the phone.

I panicked. "When does he have to see his doctor again?"

"He doesn't have to see the doctor any more."

My heart sank. "Does he know?"

"No."

I wanted to see him, one last time. I arranged to go around the following Monday, Valentine's Day. On the Sunday morning, my aunt came to visit to tell me that Billy had died the night before. Because I was afraid of my husband's reaction, I had to keep my feelings to myself all day. I waited until my husband was asleep and then I wept for my dear friend. I was determined to go to his funeral, no matter what and I enlisted the help of a friend to cover for me. I was able to see him one last time, although not the way I had wanted to. He still holds a very special place in my heart.

Seeing Billy again reminded me how someone behaves towards you when they really love you. Billy always treated me with respect. After Billy died, I became very depressed because, once again, I was hiding my feelings, keeping a secret and pretending. I was tired of pretence. I also felt more deeply than ever that my life had been a failure. I decided, about four months after Billy died, to sit down and talk to my husband about our marriage and my unhappiness. I suggested that we face facts and separate. He was furious. He threw me down, put his hands round my throat and tried to choke me with the words, "You'll never leave me, because I'll kill you first. If I can't have you, no one will." At that point I lost all hope. I had no faith in myself. I felt a complete failure and thought that no one could help me. I took an overdose of sleeping pills.

Obviously, I recovered. My husband refused to call a doctor, in case anyone would find out what I had done. Once again I was bringing shame and disgrace on the family. I left my husband then because I realised that although he said he loved me, he wasn't acting the way you do when you love someone. I stayed with some kind friends, who did arrange for a doctor to see me, but there was no real discussion about the reasons for my action and there was no suggestion of any psychological or psychiatric follow-up. Looking back, I believe that I was suffering from severe depression, as a result of the loss of my child and the failure of my marriage, as well as the loss of my dear friend, but my condition was never addressed. Also my parents had recently moved to Australia and I was feeling very lonely in my unhappy marriage without the emotional support of my mother. Perhaps I had a "nervous breakdown"; I don't know. I just know that I felt a sadness so deep that I had no hope for the future. Only many years later was I finally treated for clinical depression.

My husband apologised for his behaviour, admitted that he had been in the wrong and begged me to take him back. He promised that his behaviour would change. I decided to give him yet another chance. His behaviour did change, for a while, but not for long. Finally, three years later, he hit me again. This time was a slap across my cheek, but it was the turning point for me. It was the last straw. I decided that he had run out of chances and that he had no intention of making any permanent changes. I could tolerate his behaviour no longer. I left him for the last time. I made up my mind that I would never marry again unless I met someone who loved me the way Billy loved me.

I was married for over six years. People have asked me why I stayed married for so long. There were several reasons. I was afraid of yet another failure. My self-esteem was low. I felt that I had to give marriage every possible chance and only gave up when I was absolutely sure that there was nothing more that I could do to save the situation. Also I had to think of the children. When my husband was having one of his "good" spells, which sometimes lasted a year, he was patient and loving with the children. He happily bathed them, fed them, changed nappies, played with them and they, of course, loved him. He always saved his worst behaviour for me, although he was faithful and always worked to support us. It was hard for me to balance up my own well being with what was best for the children. Because I felt so guilty about my first son, I agonised over how to do what was best for my other four children. Ending a marriage is never a decision to be taken lightly. I desperately wanted my marriage to be a success and did manage to persuade my husband to attend marriage guidance counselling with me. He did nothing but lie. Even although he didn't tell the truth, the counsellor said at the end of the session, "Do you really think this marriage is worth saving?" What might she have said if she had known how bad things really were, I wondered. To other people, my husband was charming and affable and many people had difficulty believing that, in the privacy of our home, he was a vindictive, abusive husband. Church leaders reminded me that women should be subservient to their husbands. They made light of my suffering and made it clear that they held me responsible for the marriage break-up.

My husband did finally see a psychiatrist after we separated and she told me that if I went back to him he would make a point of making my life a misery to punish me and that, in fact, my life would be at risk. My husband had already threatened my life on several occasions. I knew already that I had no intention of going back. When I left my husband the eldest of my four children had just turned five and the youngest was five weeks old. He visited us a few times after the separation. On one of those occasions he tried to rape me. I was determined that no one was ever going to take advantage of me in that way again. I fought and kicked and he gave up. He said, "No, I wouldn't do that to you, but I would do this ...", with which he slapped me hard and knocked me across the room, "... and this ..." and slapped me hard on the other side of my face. I told him then that I wouldn't allow him in the house ever again and that if he wanted to see the children, he would have to make other arrangements. Shortly after this, he decided to go back to live in Bermuda. My mother paid for his airfare, as we had no money.

Three months later, when he received notification that I had filed for divorce, he turned up on my doorstep out of the blue, to "try to patch things up". When it became clear to him that I had no intention of reconciling, he pinned me down and attacked me viciously with his fists, punching me all over my face and head. I screamed and he picked up my daughter's nappy and held it over my nose and mouth to quieten me. I thought that I was going to suffocate. My five-month-old baby was lying beside me on the couch, mercilessly unharmed. My other three children were in another room but they came running when they heard me scream and saw their father holding the nappy over my face and telling me to "Shut up!". My younger son later amused us by saying consolingly, "At least it was a clean nappy, Mum." My husband said that he would take the nappy away if I promised to be quiet. I did. He calmed down immediately and tended to the children, who were terrified, of course. Then he began to talk about how everything was going to be all right now and we were all going to live together as a family again. He began to talk about buying new carpets. There was no apology, of course. The whole scenario was bizarre. My face was swollen and aching, one eye was closed, I had ringing in my ears and he was talking about carpets. We were in our flat and I felt that I couldn't run out and leave him with the children, as I had no idea what he might do. We had no telephone and I had no idea how to get help. I felt that I had to humour him in order to keep the children safe, but my brain was working overtime trying to work out how we could escape from him and avoid any further violence. Next thing I knew he was bringing me aspirin and telling me to rest and I would be fine.

Then there was a knock at the door. I thought that he wouldn't answer it but he did. He was so divorced from reality at this point that he actually let visitors in, apparently not realising that they would notice my injuries and take some action. It was a young couple we knew, just back from holidays, who had brought gifts for the children. They just stared at my face, looking blankly at my husband, who was acting as if everything were perfectly normal. When his back was turned, I was able to mouth to her the words, "Get your father." They made an excuse to leave as soon as possible and the children and I were left with him again. It seemed an interminable time before I heard yet another knock at the door. It was probably about half an hour. When I heard her father's voice I felt as if he had saved my life. Perhaps he did. As soon as he came in, I gathered the children together and went to a neighbour's flat to call the police. My husband was arrested and spent a few days in custody. I spent some time in hospital nursing a broken jaw. When I was released, a police officer called at my home to ask me to drop the charges. He said that he had spoken to my husband and surely I didn't want him to have a police record because, "He seemed like a reasonable sort of man."

I said to him, "Are you married?"

"Yes."

"Do you consider yourself a reasonable sort of man?"

"Yes."

"Do you do this to your wife?", indicating my bruised and swollen face.

"I take your point", was his response. My husband was duly charged. The church's response to my injury was the disparaging and inaccurate rhetorical question, "Well, there weren't actually any bones broken, were there?" I never regretted my decision to end the marriage and after the divorce I never saw my husband again. He kept in touch by mail for a few months, sending the children birthday cards (but no presents) until the divorce was finalised. After he received the court document stating that he was obliged to pay maintenance, however, we never heard from him again.

I believe that my previous experiences with men, coupled with my depression and low self-esteem related to the loss of my first child, meant that I did not have the courage to really confront the problems in my relationship with my husband very early in the marriage, when they first arose. If I had done so, much suffering could have been avoided. It seems to me ironic now that I sacrificed the right to raise my first child because I thought that he deserved two dedicated parents and yet I ended up raising my other four children alone. I was always concerned that my first son would think that I had abandoned him and then for many years I had to try to help my other four children deal with their feeling that their father had abandoned them. There have been many losses in my family.

I know that there are many men who abuse their wives, their children, their stepchildren and that for many women the solution to this problem is to choose to raise children without fathers. It takes a man and a woman to make a child, even if, in our technologically advanced society, sometimes they never actually meet each other. I believe that the solution to family abuse is to educate and encourage men to play a positive role in the lives of their partners and their children, not to try to exclude them. It is my view that to deliberately produce a child, knowing that that child will never have a relationship with his or her father, is a selfish and irresponsible act, regardless of whether the child is born to a mother on government welfare benefits or to a millionaire movie star.

After the divorce, the children and I stayed in the same little flat for two years. It was a two-bedroomed upstairs flat, hardly big enough for the five of us, especially on rainy days and there are lots of those in Renfrew. When my husband was there the children had all slept in one bedroom, but, after he left, I moved out of my bedroom and slept in my sleeping bag on the lounge room floor for two years, so that the children could have the bedrooms. Every day, in winter and often in summer too, I carried buckets of coal upstairs to light the fire to keep us warm. In winter, I often had first of all to take a kettle of boiling water down to pour over the lock on the coal bunker, to melt the snow, so that I could open it. I didn't have a car and walked most places, as it was difficult to catch public transport with children, pushchair and shopping. Money was very short and we were grateful for cast-offs from friends and neighbours. Although all the members of my immediate family were in Australia by this time, I did have aunts, uncles and cousins who were wonderful and very supportive. I also had many great friends, who visited frequently and kept my spirits up. Raising four children by myself has not been easy. It's exhausting to have to make all the decisions, to try to be fair to everyone, to have to handle everything, the discipline, the money and the squabbles. Because my husband returned, after we separated, to live in Bermuda, there were no free weekends for me while the children stayed with their father and there was no child support. I was on my own. It was hard and we were poor, but the children never went to bed hungry and we managed somehow.

Chapter 11 ... in which Evelyn moves to Australia

Two years after my marriage broke up, in 1982, I emigrated to South Australia with my four children. My parents and my brother and sister were all living there by this stage and I wanted my children to grow up within their extended family. I also wanted my children to grow up with fresh air and sunshine and birds singing. When I was eighteen, my parents had left Scotland, at the request of my sister, to live in Bermuda. After I went to live in Bermuda, they had returned to Scotland. After I returned to Scotland they moved to Australia, again at the request of my sister. When I finally arrived in Australia, I told them that they were getting too old to run away from me any more; they might as well just stay put now. They lived out their days in Australia and it is ironic that, as they grew older and became less independent, I was the one who visited them and cared for them.

    We were only able to travel to Australia through the kindness of some friends, who paid our airfares. My mother did not have enough money to transport five of us and I had barely enough money to get us to the airport, never mind half way around the world. Many years later I was able to repay them. The journey was horrendous. It lasted forty hours. I had four children under the age of seven and in the whole forty hours there was no time when they were all asleep at the same time. One vomited regularly, one had german measles (although we didn't know what was wrong with her until we arrived) and they all wriggled constantly.

Arriving in South Australia, coming back to my parents, reminded me of arriving in Bermuda. It was the same familiar pattern. Mum welcomed me while Dad glowered. The children and I had to stay with my parents until I could find a suitable place for us to live. My parents were living in a small, two-bedroomed, upstairs flat and, of course, they had no room for me, not to mention four children as well. My father made it clear that we were not welcome and had his "I might have known this would happen" expression on his face all the time. My aunt was staying with my parents on holiday at the time and so my parents had one bedroom, the four children and I had the other and my aunt slept in the lounge room. My father could not tolerate the children at all and so the five of us spent most of our time in the bedroom to avoid him. Happily, this only lasted for a few weeks and I was able to rent a house, to everyone's relief. Here I was making yet another fresh start, with only a few suitcases full of clothes and the children's favourite toys.

At the age of thirty-three, I bought my first car (second-hand, of course). It didn't last long. A young woman accidentally ran into the back of it when I was on my way to my mother's house with my four children. The children were unhurt, I had a serious whiplash injury and the car was a write-off. The only silver lining to this particular cloud was that the compensation money I received after the accident paid for the deposit on a house. At the age of thirty-four, I became a homeowner for the first time.

While I was living in Scotland, I was in fear of seeing my child somewhere. I knew that if I saw him I would want him. I used to read newspaper reports of tragedies or accidents involving children, or, worse still, of children being abused and wonder if that was my child who had suffered. I contacted the church leaders before I left Scotland to ask if all was well with my son in his adoptive family. They gave me only the briefest of information, ie that everything was fine and that there was nothing to worry about. I had no idea where he was, of course, and wasn't given any details at all about the family. I made it clear to the church leaders that I regretted having given him up and that I wanted him back. But I knew that that would only happen if something drastic happened in his adoptive family. I told them that if anything happened to his adoptive parents, if they died, or didn't want him any more, to please give him back to me. I was not encouraged to discuss the matter any further. Within a year of arriving in Australia I came to realise that the church no longer meant anything to me. Any religious feeling I had had was gone. I have had no connection with any religion since then. Christianity, in my opinion, like all religions, is a dangerous deception. Church members predicted doom and gloom when I announced that I was leaving the church and warned me that my life would be miserable and difficult without it. They couldn't have been more wrong.

In one way it was hard to leave my son behind in Scotland and travel to Australia, but in another way it meant that I no longer had to worry over every sad media report involving a child. Over the years I never forgot my first son. I thought about him constantly. Anyone who has not lost a child through adoption may find it hard to believe that I thought about him so much, but those who know will understand. I felt ashamed, guilty, sad, unworthy and frightened. I kept my feelings to myself and never talked about him. My other four children didn't know about him and my family members, who did know, never mentioned him. My first son was born on my brother's birthday and so every year when I was celebrating my brother's birthday, I was wishing I could be celebrating my son's birthday too. When the whole family was singing "Happy Birthday To You", inside I was screaming in fury, "It's my son's birthday too, you know!", but I didn't let my feelings show. I desperately wanted some acknowledgement of my first child, but I didn't expect anyone to understand and so I cried alone, just as I had done when I was pregnant. Every Christmas I was wishing that I could buy him a Christmas present. Every Mother's Day I was wondering if he would ever acknowledge me as his mother. All I could think about was whether or not I would ever see him again.

By the time I arrived in Australia, I had been lying and denying my son for twelve years. It didn't get any easier. I felt guilty and embarrassed about it all the time. A simple question like, "How many children do you have?" caused me extreme discomfort. I hated lying all the time. I was afraid to tell anyone the truth, however, as I thought that people would never understand. I couldn't understand myself how it had happened, how could I expect to be able to explain it to anyone else? Besides, I hadn't been able to bring myself to tell my other four children and so I couldn't tell anyone else until the children knew. All those years, I was in a constant state of anxiety, terrified that someone else would tell my children before I felt able to. All in all, I put myself under a lot of pressure by keeping my child a secret. It felt like a millstone around my neck. I felt like an impostor. It seemed that people did not really know me. They only thought they knew me. I was constantly afraid of being exposed for what I really was - a woman who had given away her child. I thought that if people really knew me, they wouldn't like me. I cried many more lonely tears.

I knew that under Scottish law, my son would have access to his original birth certificate when he was seventeen years old. In May 1986, when he was sixteen, I took the first step towards contacting him. I wrote to New Register House in Edinburgh to check if there had been any changes to the adoption law. They forwarded my letter to an organisation called Family Care in Edinburgh, who advised me that they had placed my name on their contact register. Family Care told me that under Scottish law there was nothing that I could do except put my name on the register and wait. They did suggest, however, that I contact the adoption agency, which had arranged the adoption, but since mine was a private adoption, arranged by the church, there was no adoption agency involved.

Somewhere, I had heard of Jigsaw, an organisation that helped family members separated by adoption. In 1989, I looked them up in the telephone directory and rang them. They referred me to ARMS SA (Inc) (which was then the Australian Relinquishing Mothers Society but is now the Association Representing Mothers Separated from their children by adoption), a support group for women who have lost children through adoption. ARMS is run by natural mothers for natural mothers. It is not run by social workers and it is not run by a government department. I cannot begin to describe how much I have gained from my association with ARMS. For the first time in a long time, at ARMS, I experienced a sense of belonging. ARMS was formed in South Australia in 1982. Since that time, natural mothers have become more and more vocal. They have lobbied for changes to the adoption legislation, which means that they now have a legal right to access information about their lost children when those children reach adulthood. They have lobbied for government funding to provide post-adoption counselling to natural mothers, which means that natural mothers can now be counselled away from the agencies that arranged the adoptions of their children. They work very hard to increase community awareness of their issues. Through ARMS I have met many women who have lost children through adoption and shared their feelings and their experiences. When I contacted ARMS I realised at last that I was not alone in my adoption experience and was finally able to share my feelings with other women who understood them. At ARMS I was able to have counselling to help me to understand how and why I lost my child. Through ARMS I've learned to channel my anger at the loss of my child into productive activities and to appreciate that my loss will always be with me.

Through ARMS, I gained the confidence to break my silence and talk about my lost child. I decided that the time had come to tell my other four children that they had a brother. I couldn't live with the fear and guilt any longer. I had no idea how they would react, but I decided that nothing could be worse than spending the rest of my life worrying about having my shameful secret exposed. They were aged nine, ten, thirteen and fourteen. I sat them down and said that I had something important to talk to them about.

My fourteen-year-old said, "It's not the birds and the bees is it, Mum?"

"Not quite", I replied.

My thirteen-year-old then surprised me by saying, "You're not going to tell us that we're all adopted, are you?"

"No", I said, "but you're getting warm."

When I did manage to tell them that I had another child, they were stunned. There was a lot of anger, there were many tears and accusations and there was little sympathy. My ten-year-old said, "Well, where is he then?" I think she thought that he was going to appear through the doorway like people do on the television show, *This Is Your Life*. When I said that I didn't know where he was, what his name was or even if he were alive or dead, they were even more upset. They said that he was part of our family and belonged with us and how could I have given him away? I tried to explain how different attitudes were all those years ago and how everyone then thought that it was the right thing to do. It was difficult for the children to imagine what it was like when I was a teenager as society had changed so much. In my teenage years there was a terrible shame attached to being pregnant and unmarried. It was an embarrassment and a disgrace. There was an expectation that couples would not have a sexual relationship until they were married. In those days they still talked about a young woman "having to" get married (ie because she was pregnant). There was tremendous pressure on unmarried mothers to give their children to married couples, because it was believed to be in the child's best interests. There was also social pressure on married couples to produce children, which created a demand for babies from infertile couples. Because in their lifetime unmarried motherhood was no longer such a disgraceful state, it was hard for my children to understand the pressure that had existed then. I think you had to be there.

They were very upset that I had deceived them and felt that they couldn't trust me and that perhaps I had kept other things from them. They thought that I should have told them when they were younger as it would have been easier for them to accept then. My problem was, of course, that when they were younger, I was not ready to tell other people about my first son. I couldn't tell my children and then ask them to keep it a secret. I couldn't tell the children until I was ready to tell everyone. They were also angry that I hadn't been able to locate him. I told them that I had been trying to find him and that I hoped that one day he would be part of our family. My nine-year-old's response to that was, "He'll probably hate you because you dumped him when he was a baby and never want to see you again. Have you thought of that?" I told her that I had thought of little else for nineteen years. She went on to say that it made her very sad to think that he might not want to meet me again, because, "If he never wants to meet you again, he'll never know what a great mum you really are." The children were desperate to find their brother and got very angry when I told them that we weren't allowed to know anything about him. They complained about how unfair it was that they couldn't contact their own brother.

Telling my other children was a painful experience, but it was also a huge relief and a very welcome release from the tyranny of deceit. I felt like someone who had been released from prison after serving a long sentence. I was finally able to be my true self after years of pretending to be otherwise. I had always encouraged them to express their feelings honestly and so I had to accept their reactions to my news. Years later the children expressed to me their sorrow that I had faced all of that sadness alone for so long before feeling ready to share it with them. I am proud of them for understanding and accepting my experience.

Through ARMS I was given the address of the National Organisation for the Counselling of Adoptees and Parents (NORCAP) in England. I wrote to them and they suggested that I write to Family Care in Edinburgh. Although I was already on the Family Care contact register, I wrote to them again to ask if there was anything else that I could do. They told me that there was no way I could get access to any information under Scottish law (natural parents apparently are not even mentioned in Scottish adoption law) and that, as my name was on the contact register, there was nothing more that I could do, just wait and hope. The attitude in Scotland seems to be that, after the adoption, natural mothers should become conveniently invisible.

Chapter 12 ... in which Evelyn tries to find her son

I was planning a trip to Scotland at the end of 1989 (also paid for by the accident compensation money) and contacted the church to ask if there were any chance of meeting my son, who was then nineteen years old, when I was there. The church leaders were actually very helpful and contacted my son's adoptive parents to explain that I would be visiting Scotland for a short time and that I probably would not be able to visit again for some years. His adoptive parents became very angry at what they viewed as intrusion and refused to even discuss the matter.

Before I went over on holiday, I did obtain a copy of my son's original birth certificate, which was wonderful. The word *Adopted* written on the bottom was like a knife through my heart. However, I felt that it belonged with me and I was very glad to have it. I enjoyed my holiday and while I was in Scotland, I spoke to some of my old friends about the attempts I had made to contact my son. After I returned to Australia, a friend sent me a newspaper cutting about an adoption agency in Glasgow called The Scottish Adoption Advice Service, which was run by Barnardo's. At first I didn't think that they could help me because they hadn't arranged the adoption of my child. I thought that because it was a private adoption, none of the adoption agencies would know anything about it.

However, I decided that it couldn't do any harm to ask them and so I wrote to them in 1990, just to ask if there was anything else that I could do to search for my son, apart from having my name on the contact register. I received a reply in December 1990 and got a huge shock. The adoption counsellor had obtained my son's adoption records and had rung his adoptive parents. I felt that she should have discussed this with me first and asked me how I wanted to proceed. She didn't know, of course, because I hadn't had a chance to tell her, that the church had already approached his adoptive parents and received a very angry reception. Of course, they were not pleased at being approached yet again and again refused to discuss the matter with him, in spite of the fact that he had not lived at home with them for some time. I will never understand why his adoptive parents, like so many others, refused to pass on my message. He was legally an adult. I know that they had no legal right and I feel that they had no moral right to keep that information from him. The adoption counsellor did tell me that my son's first name was Stephen. It was wonderful to know his name at last. The counsellor also said that his adoptive mother had described him as "a fine boy" and said that he was at university. The counsellor told me that according to Scottish adoption law, "... an adoption agency may provide such access to its case records and disclose such information in its possession as it thinks fit for the purpose of carrying out its function as an adoption agency." That is obviously very ambiguous and apparently the various adoption agencies each interpret the law in their own way. I hadn't realised that an adoption agency could access adoption records for adoptions that they had not been involved in. That was why I initially didn't go to any agencies, I tried to make contact first of all through the church.

I wrote again, in desperation, to ask if there wasn't anything at all that I could do and I received a letter dated 26 February 1991. The adoption counsellor told me that their agency had made the decision not to try to contact adopted people directly on behalf of natural parents until they reached the age of twenty-five. Even then, she said, they do not have search facilities and rely on the goodwill of the adoptive parents to inform them of the adopted person's whereabouts. My son's adoptive parents refused to tell him that I was trying to find him as they "knew" that he wasn't interested in having any contact with me. The counsellor told me that I could write to her again when my son was twenty-five, but that there was no guarantee, of course, that his adoptive parents would be any more co-operative then. The news was heart-breaking. All I had ever wanted was to contact my son and for him to have the choice of having contact with me or not.

I became very despondent, disappointed and discouraged. I felt that I had been so close, but had been prevented from taking that final step. All I could do was wait and hope that he had heard my whispered message when I held him in the hospital all those years before. I didn't have to wait very long, as it turned out. I received another letter from the same adoption counsellor dated 19 March 1991 saying, "On Wednesday 13 March a young man came to my office inquiring about his birth parents. It was Stephen." I got such a shock that I nearly dropped the letter. My first thought was that his adoptive parents had had a change of heart and decided to tell him that I was searching for him, but I was wrong. The letter went on to say, "He did not know that I had approached his mother and father." It seemed that he had heard me when I spoke to him in the hospital nursery after all.

It was a wonderful feeling to know that he had taken the initiative to try to find me. I was delirious with happiness. I felt that I had gone from the depths of despair to the heights of elation within the space of two weeks. The counsellor went on to say that she did not give him my address as she did not have my permission to do so and suggested that I either write a letter which she would pass on to him, or let her know if I wished him to write to me directly. I sent her a fax asking her to please give him my address and telephone number and ask him to call me and reverse the charges as soon as possible. He rang as soon as he heard from her. It still amazes me that a week after I received her letter, which gave me no hope at all, he was in her office with the news that I had hoped for all those years, that he wanted to contact me. I shudder when I think of how easily that contact might not have been made.

The telephone call came at about 11.30 one night when I was asleep. Although I had been anxiously awaiting a call from him, I was also afraid that it was all too good to be true and that it wouldn't happen. He didn't reverse the charges and so I suggested that I call him back. I was terrified to let him go in case something would go wrong but I wrote down his number. When I put the receiver down I was trembling. I couldn't allow any time to collect myself, however, as I was so afraid that he wouldn't be there when I rang back, or that he'd given me the wrong number, or that he wouldn't pick up the receiver. The telephone conversation lasted two and a half hours. It's a very strange experience to be asking your own child how tall he is, what colour his eyes are, what his hobbies are. I wanted to know everything about him. The first question he asked me was why I had given him up. The second was why I had never tried to find him. I heard the anger in his voice and it cut me to the quick. I panicked and thought maybe he does hate me, maybe he only wants the answers to his questions and then I'll never hear from him again. I explained to him that the church had arranged his adoption. He was not surprised and seemed, in a way, relieved. We were each equally relieved to discover that the other no longer had any connection with churches or religions. Then I explained to him that I wasn't allowed to know anything about him and that I had done all I could to try to find him. I wanted to know first of all if he had been well cared for and had a happy upbringing. I wanted to know where he had lived, where he went to school, and what did he enjoy doing, did he have close extended family and did he have a partner. He wanted to know where I was born, why was I in Australia, was I married, did I have other children, who was his father. Finally, two and a half hours later, we decided that we'd said everything we wanted to say for the time being. I was still very scared that this might be our only contact. I so much wanted to know him, to see him, to be able to explain it all to him. We agreed to write to each other and send photographs.

His first letter came and I thought, "He writes beautifully, he hasn't inherited my awful scrawl" (can you inherit untidy handwriting?). I devoured his words and examined the photographs over and over again, searching for a resemblance. In fact, we look very alike, but that wasn't clear from the photographs. I just couldn't believe my good fortune. The next step was to arrange a meeting. As I wanted him to meet the other members of my family, there was no point in considering having me go to Scotland and so we began to plan for him to come to Australia. I had missed him so much over the years, I knew that I wanted nothing more than to meet him again and I was prepared to do whatever it took to make that happen. Also I felt that I had to try to find a way to meet him while he was interested in the idea. I was still afraid if I didn't "strike while the iron was hot" that he might change his mind. I borrowed the money and the ticket was bought. The wait seemed interminable.

Chapter 13 ... in which Evelyn discovers the truth

Stephen came to Australia in September 1991 and spent three weeks with us. The other four children and I met him at the airport. It must have been a bit daunting for him to arrive and see us all lined up there. Our reunion was not tearful or demonstrative. I was battling to stay calm so as not to embarrass him. He was cool and polite. I introduced him to the other children. Looking back, I think we were both extremely brave and extremely nervous.

I was amazed to actually have him here, living in my own home. It was such a thrill to be able to introduce him to my family and friends, who all made him feel welcome. Even although my immediate family members all knew that I had had a child, no one had mentioned him over the years. I remember taking him to meet my parents. My father stood up (which was rare as he had arthritis in his knees, which restricted his mobility), extended his hand and said, "I'm very pleased to meet you." Suddenly and unexpectedly, amid my joy, I felt a surge of anger well up inside me. I wanted to shout, "Well, you weren't very pleased twenty-two years ago. You didn't make him very welcome then!", but I kept silent. I think I had spent so long hiding my feelings that it had become a habit - one that I still find it hard to break. I have no idea what my father was thinking as he met Stephen. My father and I never talked about the circumstances of Stephen's birth and he may not have been aware to what an extent he influenced my decision for Stephen to be adopted. My four legitimate children and I spent fifteen years living near my father in Australia and during that time I observed how unkindly and resentfully he treated my children. I became even more convinced that he would have treated my illegitimate child even more harshly if I had given him the opportunity.

Although I had carried the picture in my head of my first sight of my son, when he was born, somehow over the years, I had lost my picture. I was very distressed about that, as it was all I had to hold on to. I tried desperately to remember what he looked like. I felt guilty, as if I had betrayed him by forgetting. When I saw him again, at the age of twenty-one, my picture miraculously came back. It was very welcome. One of the things that he said about our reunion at the airport was the shock that he got when he saw my next eldest son. He said, "It's the first time in my life I've seen someone with my face." I showed him my class photograph, taken in my first year of primary school, in a group of about forty children. He picked me out immediately. He said, "I had the same little face when I was that age." I couldn't take my eyes off him. I wanted to look at his hands and feet, his ears, his eyes. I wanted to know about everything he had done. I froze when he told me about his appendectomy when he was twelve and how if he hadn't got to the hospital he could have died. If he had died, I would never have known and I would never have known what he had become. I wanted to watch him eat and sleep. I wanted to hear him talk and watch him walk. As soon as I saw him at the airport I saw how much he looked like me. Afterwards I kept searching for other similarities. Was he musical, did he like languages, what made him laugh? It was interesting that he wore so many earrings as it reminded me that I had had my ears pierced while I was pregnant with him. We talked about his birth. I had tried to obtain copies of my medical records from the maternity hospital. I was told that they had been destroyed. When Stephen asked for copies some years later he was told that he could have them, providing he produced a letter from his doctor. His doctor refused to provide him with a letter.

I think that my son and I are very fortunate that we are similar in many ways and we were able to establish a close relationship without much difficulty. I told him towards the end of his stay here that I had always loved him because he was my son, but it was so wonderful to get to know him and find that I actually liked him too. Like me, he has a tendency towards the unconventional and a love of travel. The relationship between a parent and a child who have been separated since the birth of the child is a unique relationship, unlike any other. It takes patience, understanding and effort on both sides, but the rewards are immeasurable. The relationship has elements of a parent-child relationship and elements of a friendship between two adults. When he was here, a friend asked us what it was like to get together again. I turned to my son and said, "Well, was it good for you?" We both smiled. Fortunately we have the same offbeat sense of humour. The other children coped well with having him here and made him feel part of the family. My youngest son was out with him on one occasion and a friend commented, "I didn't know you had another brother." My youngest son replied, "He ran away from home when he was a baby; he's just come back."

When I tell people the story of our separation and reunion, they often say how they love to hear about "a happy ending". It is happy at the moment, but it is far from being the end and while it is wonderful to have my son in my life now, his early years are lost to me forever. I didn't see him take his first step, I wasn't there for his first day at school and I didn't see him graduate from university. I haven't forgotten the agony of missing him for twenty-one years, of not knowing if he were alive or dead, of wondering if he hated me. When he left, at the end of his three-week holiday here, it was agony. Separating from him again reminded me of my original separation from him and brought back my original pain.

The telephone calls and letters continued. In 1992 he toured the United Kingdom and had a great holiday visiting friends and relatives of mine. Many of them became his friends too. I was delighted that he had made contact with some of the people who had supported me emotionally throughout my pregnancy. He came back to Australia in August 1996 for a year's working holiday, spending three months with us before travelling around the country. Saying goodbye to him yet again was a terrible wrench.

Although it's wonderful to have him in my life again, as part of my family, I realise that our reunion efforts were very "hit and miss" and could so easily have ended in disappointment for both of us. In Scotland they are proud of the fact that they were one of the few countries to have always had what they term "open adoption". What they mean by this is that adopted people in Scotland have always had access to their original birth certificates when they were aged seventeen. Sadly, however, the rights of natural parents have never been recognised under Scottish law. They have no legal right at all to any information about their lost children. Some agencies will act on behalf of natural parents to make contact with adopted, adult children. The implication is that natural mothers cannot be trusted with such information and need "responsible" people to act for them.

Gradually I learned about my son's efforts to find me. He was told that he was adopted when he was four years old and had always been curious about his origins. At the age of thirteen he found out by chance that adopted people could get access to their original birth certificates when they were seventeen and he memorised the details of how to go about doing that. He did get his original birth certificate when he was seventeen and went to an adoption counsellor to try to find me. Although my address was on his birth certificate, the flat that I was living in when he was born had been demolished. I had married overseas and had then emigrated to Australia and so really he had very little hope of ever finding me. I had no family member who shared my original surname in the Scottish telephone directory (although with a name like Burns, there would be hundreds of entries) and so he had very little to go on. He went back to the counsellor occasionally to see if they could come up with something more, but wasn't getting anywhere.

Finally, in March 1991, he decided to try yet again. He rang the adoption counsellor he had been seeing and made an appointment. The counsellor rang him back and said that he was unable to access his file because it was at another agency. My son had no idea why that would be, but he went to The Scottish Adoption Advice Service simply to get his file, to take to his own counsellor to continue his search. He was amazed when he found out the reason that they had his file was because I had been looking for him. He got upset because the counsellor refused to give him my address, as he didn't want to use an intermediary, he wanted to contact me directly. He asked if she could get him a cup of coffee and while she was out of the room he took the file out of the drawer and copied down my details. He said that he was going to allow her a week. If he hadn't heard back from her in that time, he was going to contact me himself. Of course, I got back to the counsellor the same day that I got her letter and my son and I were talking on the telephone within a very short space of time. I asked him why he hadn't put his name on the contact register and he said, "What contact register?" In spite of all his efforts to find me, no one had ever told him that a contact register even existed. If he had not decided to approach his counsellor again exactly at the time his file was with Barnardo's, he may never have known that I was searching for him. It was either an amazing coincidence or a stunning example of synchronicity. I am very proud of him for having the courage and persistence to search for me and not give up.

I find it difficult to describe the difference it has made in my life to have all five of my children around me. I don't think that anyone who has not experienced an adoption separation can truly understand the huge impact it has on a person's life. It is not an overstatement to say that my whole life was transformed when my son and I got in touch with each other. That contact put an end once and for all to my fear and ignorance about the person he had become. For Stephen, it also meant an end to fear and ignorance about the person he was. Now he knows that he was never rejected nor abandoned by me, that I did love him and that I never forgot him. Because I have researched my family history, he also has information about his ancestors going back to the middle of the eighteenth century. I was even able to tell him that I had lied to the social worker about the identity of his father and that he

90

hadn't, as he had thought, inherited his mathematical ability from his natural father.

I don't take anything for granted in our relationship. I've told him that he has no obligation to me and I appreciate that our relationship continues because we both genuinely want it to. I accept him and love him for the person that he is. In the middle of 1998 I travelled to Scotland and was finally able to fulfil my dream of being in Scotland with Stephen and going with him to the places which had been significant to me throughout my life. We went together to Renfrew and visited the site of the house in which I was born and the site of the Blytheswood School (sadly, demolished). We also travelled to Edinburgh together and I showed him where I was living when he was born and where I was when I went into labour. We even went together to the hospital in which he was born. All through these experiences I was pinching myself, as I could hardly believe that after all those years I was revisiting those places with my son. It was nothing less than a dream come true.

Leaving him again was difficult. Our separations are becoming harder for me, not easier. He now wishes to emigrate to Australia. His first application to emigrate was unsuccessful, in spite of the fact that the Department of Immigration did accept me as his sponsor as we were able to show that we are "blood relatives". He plans to re-apply.

I cannot imagine what my life would be like without him and I hope that I never have to find out.

Adoption and Loss

Part Two

The grief caused by adoption loss

Adoption and Loss

Chapter 1 Grief experienced by natural mothers

Grief is the emotional reaction to a loss. There are losses other than death which give rise to grief reactions. It is now obvious that a serious loss is experienced by the women (usually unmarried) who give birth to children who are subsequently adopted (usually soon after birth) by someone else (usually a married couple). The grief of the woman who has lost a child through adoption is a unique experience and differs in fundamental ways from other grief experiences. Although the fathers of children lost through adoption often grieve also, as do the grandparents, siblings and other members of the extended families, their grief has its own qualities and is not the same as that of the woman who has physically carried her child, given birth and signed the adoption consent form.

There is a remarkable degree of ignorance in the community and among those in the helping professions of the lifelong effect of separating a mother and child at birth. One of the reasons that the relationship between natural mothers and their adopted children has gone unrecognised is that the depth of the connection between the expectant mother and her unborn child has been underestimated. It was felt for a long time that children who were to be adopted should be removed from their mothers before a relationship between mother and child was able to develop. This attitude failed to recognise the fact that such a relationship had already developed prior to the birth of the child.

95

Many women whose children were subsequently adopted were prevented from seeing them and were sometimes lied to and told that their child had died. These actions were illegal, of course, as prior to the adoption order being granted, the natural mother was still the child's legal parent and had every right to act as such without hindrance. Natural mothers were often unaware of their legal rights, however and had been systematically disempowered throughout their pregnancies.

Until recent years, similar steps were taken in cases of stillbirth and neo-natal death. Babies were often removed before the mothers were able to see them, mothers were often not allowed to name their children and no funeral was arranged. Nowadays, women who have lost children to stillbirth or neo-natal death are encouraged to hold their children, to have photographs taken, to keep mementoes such as locks of hair and handprints, to name their children and to talk about them. Natural mothers of adopted children lack a concrete focus for their grief as most of those whose children are now adults were not allowed to see their babies prior to being separated from them and very few were allowed to touch or care for their children. Many natural mothers were not even allowed to name their babies and they were not allowed to have a birth certificate as concrete evidence that they had actually had a child. In cases of stillbirth and neo-natal death, bonding is now actively encouraged, as it is believed that this actually facilitates the grieving process. In most cases of adoption, in fact, systematic attempts were made after birth to prevent bonding, although this had already occurred regardless of these efforts. In recent times, women whose children are to be adopted have been encouraged to spend time with them before the separation, but it will be some time before it will be clear whether or not this has made any difference to the grief that they suffer.

The grief of the woman who has lost a child through adoption is one that is often not recognised by professionals such as doctors, social workers and psychologists. It is easier for them to believe that the woman acted voluntarily and therefore was comfortable with her decision. The community has often assumed that because women did not talk about their loss, that they were not suffering. Research has challenged these views and has shown that this is far from being the case. One interesting aspect of books written about natural mothers by other people, however, is that although they purport to finally tell their stories, they also go to great lengths to preserve their anonymity, thereby strengthening the notion that natural mothers should be obligingly and conveniently invisible.

Several writers have produced interesting work on the subject of natural mothers and their grief. In 1979, Joss Shawyer, a lawyer from New Zealand, wrote a book called *Death by Adoption*. In 1969, Shawyer was unmarried and pregnant with twins. She was appalled at the assumption that she would put her twins up for adoption and horrified at the pressure that was placed on her when she refused. Shawyer's book was groundbreaking as it viewed adoption as a women's issue and explored the values underpinning adoption. Shawyer describes adoption as, '... a violent act, a political act of aggression towards a woman who has supposedly offended the sexual mores by committing the unforgivable act of not suppressing her sexuality' (Shawyer, 1979, p3). According to Shawyer the punishment for this unforgivable act is, 'She is stripped of her child by a variety of subtle and not so subtle manoeuvres and then brutally abandoned' (ibid p3). Shawyer describes social workers who arranged the adoptions as, 'Specially trained state-employed personnel ... (who) ...police her fall from grace and arrange to remove the product of her transgression to a safe and secret place' (ibid p3). Shawyer describes how immature, unmarried mothers were persuaded to allow their children to be given to infertile, married women, supposedly "for their own good". Shawyer tells the stories not just of natural mothers, but also of adopted people. Her book also includes an interview with an adoptive mother and an interview with an involuntarily childless woman who did not adopt. Their stories are riveting, although often tragic.

Phyllis Silverman is the author of a book entitled *Helping Women Cope with Grief* (1981). This is one of a few books that actually tackle the issue of the grief of natural mothers directly. In the introduction to her book, she points out that she is addressing the issues of women who have found themselves in situations, '... for which their previous experience has not prepared them' (Silverman, 1981, p9). Her book is directed at those in the helping professions. Silverman challenges the stereotype of the very young, uneducated, natural mother and quotes a study of women who had lost children through adoption which took place in North Carolina in the early 1960s. This study showed that, '... half of them were over 21 years of age, 70% of them had finished at least high school, and the vast majority of them had been going with their babies' fathers for at least six months' (ibid p58). Silverman describes how so many natural mothers suppressed their grief and how this suppressed grief manifested itself, in feelings of guilt, anger, tenseness and fear of discovery (ibid p60). Silverman goes on to say that, '... the pain, secrecy and guilt involved in their experience can profoundly affect their future marriages' (ibid p61). Silverman also points out that some natural mothers later marry in order to gain approval from parents, who, '... had expressed disappointment or disgust with their previous pregnancies' (ibid p61). Silverman describes the impact of breaking the secrecy as a 'thawing out' as natural mothers sometimes describe themselves after disclosing their status, '... as having been in a deep freeze, sometimes for years' (ibid p66). Silverman acknowledges the crucial importance of support groups for natural mothers and says that, 'Without such an understanding and sympathetic forum, many birthmothers would remain in hiding, postponing or even indefinitely deferring their accommodation to their grief' (ibid p69).

Among those who have addressed the grief and loss issues of women who have lost children through adoption are Robin Winkler and Margaret van Keppel. Winkler and van Keppel presented a paper at the Third Australian Adoption Conference in 1982. In this paper they compared the loss of a child through adoption with other losses and pointed out its two main distinguishing features (Winkler & van Keppel, 1982, p175). The first is the fact that the natural mother feels responsible for the decision to give up the child for adoption and therefore feels the loss as a self-inflicted one. This results in feelings of guilt, shame and powerlessness. The second is that the child is lost to the mother but still lives and so there is always the possibility of a reunion. This means that there is a lack of finality to the loss. These are the two most important factors, which make resolution of the natural mother's grief exceptionally difficult.

In 1984, Winkler and van Keppel conducted a study of two hundred and thirteen women, Australia-wide, who had lost a first child through adoption (Winkler & van Keppel, 1984). They found that the effects of the loss of the child on the mother were both negative and long lasting. All of the women who participated in the study reported a sense of loss, which did not diminish over time. In fact, approximately half of the women surveyed reported an increase in the sense of loss over time. The women surveyed, compared with a comparison group, had significantly more problems of psychological adjustment. The women involved in the Winkler and van Keppel study were, of course, all volunteers, most of whom responded to requests in the media. Natural mothers such as these, who are prepared to discuss their experiences and feelings, have obviously already made some adjustment to their situation compared to those who have not yet addressed their loss issues and are still operating under the burden of silence and suppression. Since the women involved in the study stated that their sense of loss had not decreased, which is what one would expect to happen in most cases of loss, then the many natural mothers who did not volunteer to participate in the study could be expected to be experiencing more serious negative, long-term effects related to the loss of their children through adoption.

In 1984 also, Kate Inglis wrote a book called *Living Mistakes*, which is sub-titled, *Women who consented to adoption* (Inglis, 1984). Her book grew out of her observation that women who were recounting their reproductive histories and revealed that they had lost a child through adoption, '... exhibited a pattern of behaviour in the telling which centred on an unresolved grief and an ambivalence about their motherhood' (Inglis, 1984, p18). Inglis goes on to say that, 'Their isolation in both the event and the memory was striking'. Inglis states that while anger is a common response to loss and a recognised component of grief, 'Anger is also a likely consequence following relinquishment' (ibid p170). She goes on to describe many of the ways in which natural mothers are angry and many of the ways in which that anger can be expressed. She also acknowledges that in many cases it remains unexpressed. Inglis says of the natural mother, 'She may begin her pregnancy in anger and resentment and continue for years with a randomly placed rage' (ibid p170).

Dr John Condon of Flinders Medical Centre, South Australia, conducted some research in 1986. The results of his South Australian study of twenty natural mothers support Winkler and van Keppel's conclusions. Condon found, '... a very high incidence of pathological grief reactions which have failed to resolve although many years have elapsed since the relinquishment' (Condon, 1986, p117). Condon also recorded that more than half of the women he surveyed reported that their anger had increased since the time of relinquishment (ibid p118). This was further evidence that not only was time not leading to the resolution of grief for natural mothers, but that the passage of time was in most cases actually exacerbating their condition.

At a conference in 1987, van Keppel, Midford and Cicchini presented a paper in which they pointed out that there were often additional stressful life-events connected with the loss of a child through adoption (van Keppel, Midford & Cicchini, 1987, p44). Many natural mothers had to move to another residence or sometimes to another town during their pregnancy in order to avoid the shame and embarrassment for themselves and their families. For many, the pregnancy meant the end of their relationship with the father of their child. Some were forced by the pregnancy to leave study or employment. The pregnancy caused an irreversible change in the relationship between the natural mother and her parents, whether the parents were aware of the pregnancy or not. The pregnancy often drove a wedge between the expectant mother and her friends. Natural mothers often resented their friends for their freedom and their hopes for the future. As a result of these changes, many natural mothers felt very isolated at the time of their pregnancies. Most natural mothers were immature and unable to cope with this combination of stressful events all occurring at the same time. After enduring the pregnancy, often in social isolation, they were then required to make a decision regarding their child's future. Van Keppel, Midford and Cicchini note that, 'It is not uncommon for birth mothers to experience difficulties in forming or maintaining significant relationships' and they relate this to the fact that the relinquishment of the child was coupled with other traumatic events (ibid p45).

In the last decade two books in particular have drawn attention to the issues of women who have lost children through adoption in the United Kingdom. In 1991, Patricia Bouchier, Lydia Lambert and John Triseliotis wrote a book called *Parting with a child for adoption, the mother's perspective*. The book was published by the British Agencies for Adoption and Fostering, an organisation which arranges adoptions. The women who were interviewed for the book were mostly mothers who had registered with Birth Link, the contact register managed by Family Care, in Edinburgh. The original intention of the authors was to test certain hypotheses, which included the following; *the less counselling and family support the mother received at relinquishment over her experience and loss, the more likely it is that she will now be seeking information or reunion rather than showing no interest in either* and *unresolved feelings of grief and guilt are likely to correlate with the absence of counselling and wider family support at the time of relinquishment* (Bouchier, Lambert & Triseliotis, 1991, pp11-12). The implication obviously is that if only the women involved had been adequately counselled at the time that they were separated from their children, they would not in later years be experiencing feelings of unresolved grief and they would not be interested in being reunited with their children. The authors seem to believe that if only professionals could find the "right" way to take women's children from them, then there would be no need to provide any further services to these women and they would conveniently disappear from the picture, never to be seen or heard of again. In fact, they were unable to test these hypotheses, as there was very little evidence of any counselling at all being provided at the time of separation of mother and child. The grief of the mothers and their desire to be reunited with their children appear to be viewed by the authors as unfortunate outcomes of the lack of counselling and family support at the time of the separation. *In fact, in my view, they are a healthy, appropriate response to the loss of a child.* I believe that there is no "right" way to separate a mother and child by adoption and that the mother and child will always suffer, regardless of what attempts are made to make the experience less traumatic. It will always be difficult for natural mothers to resolve their grief because they will always be viewed as having acted voluntarily (this is even more relevant in our time as there are so many more options open to unmarried, pregnant women now than there were several decades ago) and there will always be a lack of finality to their grief as there will always be the possibility of reunion (this is also much more likely in our time than in previous decades). Bouchier et al stated in 1991 that, 'In contrast to other western countries (New Zealand, Australia, Canada and the United States), social work agencies in Britain have not yet addressed many of the issues raised by birth mothers in this and other studies' (Bouchier et al, 1991, pp 106-107). There is no evidence, unfortunately, that this situation has improved since that date.

Then, in 1992, David Howe, Phillida Sawbridge and Diana Hinings wrote a book called *Half a Million Women - Mothers who lose their children by adoption.* In this book they explore the grief experienced by natural mothers and describe the experiences of natural mothers who attended support groups at the Post Adoption Resource Centre in London. All three of the authors have previously worked in the area of arranging adoptions, however and make it clear that they are in favour of adoption continuing. While they recognise the grief of natural mothers and describe it in detail and with some insight, they seem to consider it a necessary evil and a problem to be simply tolerated.

Although some useful work has been done in the exploration of the grief of natural mothers, those who have written about natural mothers are most often academics or social workers. They purport to focus on the point of view of the natural mother but, in fact, they usually write about natural mothers from the point of view of those who are part of the system that created the mothers' grief in the first place. Like Howe et al they usually support adoption and are prepared to accept that more and more women will lose their children in this way. Although they do consider useful ways to assist natural mothers with grief resolution, they seem to be blinded to the fact that their pain has been caused by adoption and that there will only be an end to the pain of natural mothers when there is an end to adoption. They view the pain of natural mothers as inevitable, as they see adoption as inevitable. It is difficult for natural mothers to have confidence in authors who describe adoption as being '... highly prized as a way of caring for children who cannot be brought up by the parents to whom they were born' (Howe et al, 1992, p99). Attitudes like this among professionals in the so-called helping professions will perpetuate the grief and loss experienced by the natural mothers of adopted children and reflect the uninformed, outdated social system which created that grief in the first place.

When support groups are mentioned by Howe et al, for example, there is often the assumption that the women who attend are those who have not had a good experience with adoption and that those who do not attend are happy with their adoption experience. No evidence is provided to support this hypothesis, however. In my view this is an insulting and dangerous assumption and, based on my experience, totally incorrect.

All of the research that has been performed among the natural mothers of adopted children has shown that they carry their grief with them for many years and that it does not evaporate over time. Howe et al refer to Winkler and van Keppel's research when they point out that some women, '... felt they had accepted the loss only to find that years later the feelings of unresolved grief returned' (Howe et al 1992, p83). Results highlight the anger and sense of loss experienced by natural mothers and the fact that these can often actually increase with the passage of time.

There is still a lot that could be learned about the effects of adoption on the lives of natural mothers. Some who have tried to gauge how well women have recovered from the loss of their children have made the mistake of trying to make an assessment much too early. It is not possible, in my opinion, to judge how well or how badly women have adjusted to the loss of their children at least until those children have reached adulthood. Anecdotal evidence suggests that women's feelings are different when their children are still minors, compared to when their children reach adulthood. When the children are still legally under age, then natural mothers are very aware that someone else has parental rights over their children. During this period, natural mothers tend to be rather tentative and hesitant about their feelings towards their children. There is also an element of self-protection. It is a more attractive option to comfort themselves with the idea that they have done the right thing, while there is still no possibility of having to justify their position to their adult children. Once those children are adults, however and parental rights are no longer an issue, they know that they have as much legal right as anyone else does to have a relationship with that person and this knowledge affects their outlook.

It would be useful to know, for example, how many natural mothers went on to marry the father of their lost child and what impact the loss of the child had on the relationship, how many of them (apparently almost half) suffered from secondary infertility after losing their first (and only) child, how many natural mothers have suffered from cancer in middle age (anecdotal evidence suggests a higher percentage than is evident in the general community), what impact did their relationships with their parents have on their attitude to adoption and what difference has access to information and actual reunion made to grief resolution? Unfortunately, there seems to have been a reluctance to perform such research. Further research in all of these areas would be very valuable.

Chapter 2 Grief experienced by adopted people

Until recently, very little attention was paid to the grief experienced by adopted people. Some references have been made to adoptions which had unhappy outcomes for the adopted children, for example where the adoption was terminated by the adoptive parents and the child returned to care, or where the child was abused by the adoptive parents. These unhappy situations are more common than many people would like to admit. In many cases, however, the painful consequences of adoption are less obvious. Only in recent years has come the realisation that adopted people, regardless of how apparently problem-free their adoptions have been, experience a deep and painful sense of loss because they have been separated from their natural mothers. Their grief resulting from this loss is not always obvious because it has usually been suppressed and is often exhibited indirectly in the behaviour of adopted people, especially in the adolescent years. If the grief is not addressed appropriately, however, the behaviours can continue on into adulthood. Adopted people, like their natural mothers, have not been encouraged by society to express their grief as the expectation was that they would be grateful to their adoptive parents for "rescuing" them. Society has traditionally admired adoptive parents for doing what appeared to be a community service by adopting children who were thought to be without families. In fact, these children did have families and they suffered from having spent their lives

105

separated from them. We are now aware that most natural mothers give up their children very reluctantly, under the impression that they are giving up their right to raise them in order to benefit the children.

For many adopted people, the fact that they were not raised by their natural mothers causes them to feel rejected and abandoned. They suffer from the loss of their relationship with their natural mothers, the loss of kinship by being separated from their extended family and community and the loss of identity from not knowing exactly who they are. These losses are particularly obvious in the cases of cross-cultural adoptions. This was very poignantly illustrated by Dr Joyce Maguire Pavao at the Adoption and Healing Conference in New Zealand in 1997. Dr Pavao is an adopted person and a family therapist. She told the story of a young man called Trevor who attempted suicide when he was thirteen years old. Trevor had been adopted from Colombia when he was four years old by an American family, described by Pavao as, '... very affluent, a white family who lived in a beautiful suburb of Boston'. Dr Pavao tried to help the young man find a reason to go on living. His response to her was, 'You don't understand, Joyce, I can't live. I'm dead. I have been dead since I was four or five years old. My name was Ricardo. I spoke Spanish. I lived in another country, I was another person and I have been trying very hard to be this new person and I can't do it, I just can't do it.' (Pavao, 1997, p200).

Our society has found it difficult to accept that adoption has caused more problems than it has ever solved and there is still a great deal of resistance in the community to acknowledging the damage caused by adoption. Fortunately, more and more research is being done, however, on the outcomes for adopted people, although even those who have exposed the unhappy results of adoption have difficulty understanding that the pain caused to adopted people is not inevitable and that society does not simply have to tolerate it.

Adopted people, like natural mothers, lack a concrete focus for their grief, as they usually have no conscious memory of their natural mothers. There is also no finality to their grief, as they know that they have another family somewhere and that they will always, in some way, be a part of that family. Adopted people lack any rituals to facilitate their grieving, as they were usually not intellectually aware at the time that the adoption took place and there is always an element of secrecy about their origins. Even if they are told that they are adopted, many questions and mysteries remain. Like their natural mothers, they have often not expressed their true feelings of loss and so too often the assumption has been that those feelings did not exist. As their natural mothers appeared to "get on with their lives" and often showed no outward signs of their inner turmoil, so adopted people often appear to be content with their lot and show no obvious signs of grieving. This does not mean, of course, that they do not suffer.

An article called *The Painful Legacy of Adoption* appeared in The Age newspaper in Melbourne, in June 1993. It was written by Louise Bellamy. Ms Bellamy reported that she had interviewed Brother Alex McDonald who had worked with homeless young people in St Kilda in Melbourne for ten years. Ms Bellamy reported Brother McDonald as saying that, '... of the 147 suicides of young people caused by drugs and abuse in the area over the past decade, 142 came from adoption backgrounds' (Bellamy, 1993). This article should have promoted a national outcry and further investigation of these horrific statistics. The fact that it did not is further evidence of the reluctance in the community to acknowledge the emotional damage that has been caused to adopted people.

Nancy Verrier is an adoptive mother and a clinical psychologist. She presented a paper at the American Adoption Congress International Convention in 1991 and later expanded it into a book called *The Primal Wound* (Verrier, 1993). Verrier spoke at the convention of the 'staggering' statistics which show that although adopted people make up 2-3% of the population in the United States, they make up 30-40% of the young people in 'special schools, juvenile hall and residential treatment centres' (Verrier, 1991). In this paper, Verrier described how the adopted person's perception of having been abandoned by their natural mother affects their feelings of self-worth in a negative way and causes them to have a constant fear of further abandonment. Verrier explained that this fear of abandonment results in hyper-vigilance on the part of the child, which is why so many adopted people suffer from free-floating anxiety and psychosomatic illnesses, especially unexplained stomach-aches, headaches and allergies. Verrier spoke of the separation of the child from the natural mother as an experience 'from which neither fully recovers' and said that the adopted person, in losing the sense of well being and security of the presence of their original mother, had 'lost something which could never be regained'. Verrier also spoke about the phenomenon of adopted people sabotaging their birthdays, because the anniversary for them represents sorrow and parting, not joy. In this paper, Verrier also explained that adopted people often apparently make a 'good adjustment' to their adoption, but what this means is simply that they learn how to seek approval and to suppress their true feelings.

Verrier wrote in 1993 of the pain experienced by adopted people and of the difficulties of finding professionals who are aware of the issues for adoptive families. In *The Primal Wound* (1993), Verrier describes how many adoptive parents believe that all their adopted children need is to be loved and how, as adopted children grow up, parents often have difficulty understanding their testing-out behaviour. One of the reasons that there has been little recognition of the needs of adopted people is the lack of understanding of the bond between mother and child which grows during pregnancy and the resultant impact on the child of the separation from the mother. Some adoptive parents who have never had natural children of their own find it difficult to understand the importance of this bond. Verrier, however, has had her own natural child and so perhaps this has made it easier for her to appreciate the bond that develops during pregnancy. Verrier also explains that she finally came to understand that it is sometimes difficult for adopted children to accept the love that their adoptive parents want to give them and that this testing-out behaviour is, '... one of two diametrically opposed responses to being abandoned, the other being a tendency toward acquiescence, compliance and withdrawal' (Verrier, 1993,

Preface). Verrier says that it sometimes takes years of therapy for adopted people to get in touch with their feelings of rejection. Verrier found that adopted people were, 'greatly over-represented in psychotherapy', that they '...demonstrated a high incidence of juvenile delinquency, sexual promiscuity and running away from home' and that they consistently showed symptoms which were 'impulsive, provocative, aggressive and antisocial' (ibid).

Verrier writes about the difference between attachment and bonding. She says that adopted children form an attachment to their adoptive parents because they quickly come to realise that their survival depends on it, but that they may never truly bond with them (Verrier, 1993, p19). Verrier points out that bonding begins in the womb and is exhibited by the fact that, in the crucial period immediately following birth, new-born babies have been shown to recognise their mothers, through smell, heartbeat, voice and eye contact. The child is born with the expectation that its life will revolve around the person with whom it has become familiar for nine months. When this does not happen, when this continuum is broken by the child suddenly being handled by a different person ie the adoptive mother, the baby can be left feeling, '... hopeless, helpless, empty, and alone' (ibid p21). Verrier goes on to say that, in her opinion, '... the severing of that connection ... causes a primal or narcissistic wound ... which manifests in a sense of loss, basic mistrust, anxiety and depression, emotional and/or behavioural problems, and difficulties in relationships with significant others' (ibid p21).

Betty Jean Lifton is an adopted person and the author of several books on adoption topics. In 1994, Lifton wrote *Journey of the Adopted Self*, in which she explores the impact of adoption on adopted people. Lifton also describes the two opposing responses of adopted people, which are particularly noticeable during adolescence, when she describes the compliant adopted people who, because of their issues of unresolved grief and loss, '... pay the price with eating disorders, phobias, and an underlying depression' while others, '... take an oppositional stance to anyone who tries to control them, be they parents, school teachers, or legal authorities' (Lifton, 1994, p66). In many families where there are two adopted children, it is common for one child to be compliant and the other to be rebellious. This was described to me by one adoptive mother as, "One shuts up, the other acts up."

Lifton goes on to say that adopted children, '... often do not feel entitled to express any negative feelings, such as grief or anger at being cut off from their origins' (Lifton, 1994, p30) and points out that this anger often displays as depression (ibid p89). It also, however, often, 'manifests itself in destructive, acting-out behaviour' (ibid p91). Lifton gives as a possible cause of the over-representation of adopted people in psychiatric wards, '... the difficulty many young adoptees have repressing their grief and anger and sense of powerlessness' (ibid p91) and says, 'Therapists should not be asking why adopted children are angry, but why shouldn't they be?' (ibid p89). Lifton also points out that many adoptive parents find these ideas threatening. She says, 'The need to idealize the institution of adoption in order to ward off their own fears unfortunately prevents these parents from being in touch with their children's pain' (ibid p91).

Lifton also writes about the trauma associated with adoption and the, '... high psychic cost that both parent and child pay when they repress their grief and loss' (Lifton, 1994, p8). She goes on to say that, in her opinion, '... it is unnatural for members of the human species to grow up separated from ... their natural clan' and that because of the effects of this separation on adopted people, 'They grow up feeling like anonymous people cut off from the genetic and social heritage that gives everyone else roots' (ibid p8). Lifton is aware that this news is not often well received by adoptive parents. She cautions them that if they love their children they will have empathy for the sorrow that they experience not, '... turn on the professionals who describe it' (ibid p33). Lifton writes about adopted people being 'strong enough' to claim their heritage (ibid p47), when they search for their natural mothers and describes how in children who have been adopted, lack of knowledge about their origins 'interferes with the child's struggle to form an early sense of self' and that '... not even the most loving adoptive parents ... can soften the psychic toll that ...

exacts from the child' (ibid p49). Lifton describes how an Artificial Self is created. She describes the Artificial Self as being '... compliant, afraid to express its real feelings, such as sadness or anger, for fear of losing the only family it has' (ibid p52). In fact, Lifton suggests that the suffering of adopted children may begin before they are even born. Research now suggests that unborn children respond to sound and may be affected by the experiences and emotions of their mothers during pregnancy. Many natural mothers will respond emotionally to Lifton's rhetorical question, 'Does the fetus get a physiological message of its dark fate from the turbulent wrenching of the womb as its mother's body lies convulsed with grief?' (ibid p30).

Lifton describes separation anxiety and how it exists in adoptive families. Many adopted people have difficulty separating from their adoptive parents, even to attend school. The reason these difficulties arise is that any separation resurrects the feelings of loss related to the original separation from the natural mother. Lifton also says that some adopted people deliberately choose to become indispensable to their adoptive parents to ensure that they will not be abandoned by them and therefore not have to undergo yet another separation (Lifton, 1994, p70). Children were often adopted to fulfil the desires and fantasies of their adoptive parents. Many adopted people, even into adulthood, feel an unhealthy responsibility for ensuring that their adoptive parents are happy. Some never outgrow the compliant attitude they practised as they were growing up. For other adoptees, the search for an identity leads them to choose a negative identity in order to associate with the impression they have obtained from their adoptive parents that their original parents were somehow defective (ibid p71).

Both Lifton and Verrier mention the fact that sexual promiscuity is common among adopted people. Lifton says, 'Both male and female adoptees give themselves freely to others out of a sense of worthlessness or as a way of trying to get close to another person. Physical intimacy gives them the illusion of love' (Lifton, 1994, p72). Lifton also mentions David Kirschner, who, she says, found that adopted people often exhibited, '... deceptive charm that covered over a shallowness of attachment' (ibid p92).

Joanne Small is an adopted person and a clinical social worker. She is the author of an article entitled, *Working with Adoptive Families*, which was published in a journal called *Public Welfare* in 1987. The article is sub-titled, *We must come to see that families who adopt are not the same as others*. Small describes how adoptive families operate to deny the difference between raising adopted children and raising one's own natural children. A result of this denial, according to Small, is that, '... the child's basic sense of self develops around a faulty belief system' (Small, 1987, p36). This is obviously damaging to the developing child who is trying to establish his or her identity and place in the family and in the world. Small describes some of the characteristics of adoptive families, for example, family members have difficulty identifying and expressing their feelings about adoption, there is a tendency toward perfectionism and unrealistic expectations, fantasy replaces reality, there are feelings of powerlessness, members of the family feel responsible for the feelings of others, members of the family share low self esteem and family members show a strong need for approval (ibid p36). Adopted children may sometimes be high achievers academically, but this certainly does not indicate that they do not suffer emotionally.

Small writes about the confusion created in the minds of adopted children who are told by their adoptive parents that their natural mothers gave them away because they loved them. Children know that people do not give away that which they value. When their adoptive mothers then tell them that they love them also, there is an underlying fear that they too may one day give them away. Who would say, for example, "I love my husband/wife so much that I'm going to give him/her to you"? It makes no sense. How then, do we expect children to accept that it was because their mothers loved them so much that they gave them away to other mothers to raise?

Small also describes the denial which exists among professionals who work with adopted people of the importance in their lives of having been adopted. Small says, 'We must recognize the role of denial among professionals working with adoptive families, some of whom are themselves members of adoptive families and many of whom are unwittingly engaged in codependent roles' (Small, 1987, p41). Small calls for training to be provided to professionals, which should include, '... an understanding of the differences in adoptive family structure, the role of denial in adoptive families, the meaning and effects of codependence on professionals and adoptive family members' among other factors (ibid p41). Small describes the denial practised by adopted people. She says, 'Adult children of adoption also carry with them a strong tendency to deny that adoption can be the basis for their problems' (ibid p40). Small goes on to describe how adopted people can let go of this denial by searching for their natural mothers. Small says that, 'Adult children who search have chosen to give up the denial' (ibid p40). Small recommends that adopted people attend support groups in order to share their experiences and gain strength from the support of others who have also been adopted. In this way their innermost feelings can be validated and not denied.

In some countries, it sometimes happens that, after a marriage, a stepparent adopts a child of his or her partner. In most cases, the natural parent, with whom the child no longer lives, signs an adoption consent. In all cases, as with all adoptions, the child's name is changed. Many children who have been adopted by stepparents have the same sorts of issues that other adopted children have. They have a parent who has lost the right to parent them and they have grown up with at least one parent to whom they are not genetically related. Children adopted by stepparents have also been issued with a new, false birth certificate and have lost their original identities. Some of them have issues of abandonment and low self-esteem. Some have issues of identity and belonging. There is no justification for stepparent adoptions. Matters of inheritance can be resolved by the making of a will and an adoption does not necessarily guarantee that a child will feel welcome in the newly created family. Fortunately, the passing of the Adoption Act (1988) in

South Australia virtually put an end to stepparent adoptions. Sadly, stepparent adoptions are still common in the United Kingdom.

While there is no avoiding the fact that adopted people are more likely to find themselves in psychiatric care, there is no way of knowing for sure why this is so. Some adoptive parents blame it on heredity, although anecdotal evidence suggests that subsequent children raised by natural mothers do not require psychiatric help to the same degree. Some put it down to the fact that adoptive parents are more inclined to introduce their adopted children to psychiatric interaction, because they are ambivalent about raising someone else's child, have not come to terms with their infertility or are disappointed in the child for not being the ideal child that they had hoped for. While these factors may go some way towards explaining the over-representation of adopted people in psychiatric care, they certainly do not explain the over-representation of adopted people in the prison system, among youth suicides and among the homeless. Considering what we know about attachment and identity, it is far more likely that the behaviours of adopted people are a reaction to the losses that they have experienced.

Research undertaken among adopted people shows that they grieve for the loss of their mothers and their natural families and that this grief affects their feelings of self-worth and their ability to form close relationships with other people. Anecdotal evidence suggests that there is a high number of adopted women who subsequently lose their own children through adoption. Anecdotal evidence also suggests that there are additional issues for adopted people who discover that their original parents actually married after their adoption. There must be an end to the denial surrounding the damage caused by adoption in order that adopted people can receive appropriate help which acknowledges their grief and loss and supports them to work towards resolution.

Chapter 3 Grief counselling

Having established that natural mothers and adopted people do grieve after their separation, it might be expected that they could be assisted by grief counselling. Much has been written about grief, its purpose and its expected course. For most people grief following a loss, such as a death, is productive ie it leads to resolution. In many cases grief counselling can be helpful in assisting people to come to terms with their loss. Suggestions for grief counselling are provided by Worden in his book *Grief Counselling and Grief Therapy* (Worden, 1982). Other writers on the topic offer similar advice for assisting those who are grieving. Worden believes that mourning is necessary after a loss in order to re-establish equilibrium and describes the four tasks which he believes should be completed in order to achieve the emotional healing which should follow mourning (Worden, 1982, pp11-16).

The first task described by Worden is acceptance of the reality of the loss. This is a difficult task for natural mothers, as they often do not have any concrete focus for their grief. Many of them did not see their babies and after being separated from them they were given no formal acknowledgement of the child's birth or adoption. The denial practised by society in general of their experience and their existence also lends an air of unreality to the event. The fact that, in many cases, their child is issued with a new, false birth certificate, which denies the existence of the original parents, is an example of this communal denial. Those who grieve a death must accept the irreversibility of the loss, but natural mothers often dream that their child will return to them. This makes it difficult for them to accept the reality of the loss because they can never be quite sure whether or not it is irreversible.

Accepting the reality of the loss is difficult for adopted people as they also lack a concrete focus for their grief. They have no conscious memory of what they have lost in terms of their mother. What they have lost in terms of a possible life can only be guessed at, not measured. They have lost the possibility of being raised in their natural family, but who is to know what that might have been like? The very fact that adoption agencies often tried to "match" adopted children with the physical characteristics of the adoptive parents suggests that the intention was to facilitate a denial of the truth. Presented with a new birth certificate and a new identity, adopted people are unable to conceptualise the lost person, the person they would have been. Like their mothers, adopted people are aware that the lost family exists somewhere and so their loss, like that of their natural mothers, is not final.

Worden's second task is that of experiencing the pain of grief. Worden states that if this pain is avoided or suppressed then the course of mourning will be prolonged. Worden also says that avoidance of conscious grieving often leads to depression (Worden, 1982, p14). Because natural mothers are viewed as voluntarily giving up their children, their grief is not socially recognised and supported, they are not given permission to mourn at the time of their loss and so their grieving is usually postponed. Many natural mothers are surprised at the depth of their pain many years after the event, when they are finally allowed to express their grief.

Adopted people are often expected to be grateful for being adopted and "rescued" from their unhappy situation. When they speak up about their losses, which more and more of them are now finding the courage to do, they are often unjustly labelled "ungrateful" and "disloyal". Many babies do, indeed, exhibit grief reactions at the time of their adoption, but there is also a need for adopted adults to be permitted to understand their loss and to actually experience their grief.

Worden's third and fourth tasks are closely connected. The third task is that of adjusting to the environment from which the lost person is missing and the fourth task is to withdraw emotional energy and reinvest it in another relationship. For natural mothers the place of their lost child in their environment is one of expectation. The expectant mother is physically and emotionally prepared to take up the role of motherhood and to the mother whose child is adopted by someone else this role is denied. Natural mothers try to adjust to this fact in different ways. Many of them have another child, or other children, to try to fill the gap created by the lost child. Many natural mothers, however, perhaps as many as 40%, are unable to have any further children. They sometimes fear that another emotional attachment may also result in loss. Some feel that having given up one child, it would be disrespectful and disloyal to that first child to then have another child, which is not given up. Some respond to their loss by distancing themselves from babies and young children, others take every opportunity to spend time with other people's babies. Natural mothers live with the contradiction that they are mothers but not mothers. They know that they have had a child but they are expected to go on with their lives as if that child had not been born.

Adopted people vary in the ways in which they adjust to their new environment after adoption. Some try very hard to please, in order to feel safe in their relationship with their adoptive parents. Others are so afraid of further abandonment that they do not allow themselves to become close to anyone, thus protecting themselves from further hurt.

Natural mothers and adopted people are unable to perform the sorts of tasks that are expected following a loss, in order for grief resolution to proceed. It is obvious, therefore, that the standard formulae for grief counselling are not going to be appropriate for them. This does not mean, however, that they cannot be helped.

Kenneth Doka is the editor of a book entitled, *Disenfranchised Grief*, which is subtitled, *Recognizing Hidden Sorrow* (1989). This book is very useful for those trying to understand grief caused by adoption. In this book, David Meagher says that, '... the most difficult loss to support occurs when the assumption is made that people who make anomalous life choices ... do not deserve support' (Meagher, 1989, p313). Natural mothers are very aware that for many people, the choice to give away one's baby is certainly considered an anomalous life choice and that, as a result of this judgment, many people, including those in the helping professions, are unable to give emotional support to natural mothers. For this reason many natural mothers refuse to consult professionals for assistance with their grief resolution. Instead they choose to attend a mutual aid self-help organisation and for them the first step towards resolution of their grief is to be able to discuss it in a supportive and accepting environment such as this. For many the loss of their child has been a taboo subject for many years and they experience a huge sense of relief at being able to acknowledge the child and the adoption. Because of the lack of understanding in the community of the issues of adopted people, they also benefit from the support of a self-help organisation.

Some natural mothers, however, do consult professionals and request assistance in resolving their grief. Van Keppel, Midford and Cicchini believe that there are ways for professionals to promote the adjustment of women who have lost children through adoption. They suggest that grief counselling can be useful to natural mothers and that this needs to be provided in an atmosphere of compassion and acceptance (van Keppel, Midford & Cicchini, 1987, p46). They stress the importance of natural mothers being given permission to express their feelings. In order for adopted people to be really in touch with their feelings of loss and grief, they have to break out of their denial and challenge the belief that adoption solved their "problem". Meagher points out that, 'Grief that is absent, masked, or suppressed is abnormal and becomes pathological' (Meagher, 1989, p313). It is important for those in the helping professions to be aware, when working with natural mothers and adopted people, that in many cases their grief has been suppressed for many years and may, in fact, have become pathological. For this reason, it is unreasonable to expect short-term resolution.

Grief counselling can be very useful in helping natural mothers to sort out where the responsibility lies. They can be assisted to explore to what extent they were responsible for the loss of their children and to what extent others were responsible. With a better understanding of the pressures and motives involved, they can take responsibility for their own behaviours and realise that they are not responsible for the behaviours of others. Anger is a common component of grief. Natural mothers need to be assured that their anger is justified and encouraged to express it in appropriate and productive ways. Productive expression of anger often leads to valuable changes being made.

There are also implications for the care of natural mothers and adopted people who experience other losses in their lives. Because their adoption loss remains unresolved, they often have great difficulty dealing with subsequent losses. Bereavement counsellors report that often those who are displaying lack of adaptation to a loss have, in fact, experienced a previous loss which remains unresolved, often because their grief in that previous situation was disenfranchised for some reason. Those who counsel the bereaved report that they often find that women who are having difficulty coming to terms with a death will eventually admit to having previously experienced the loss of a child through adoption. The lack of resolution of this previous loss impedes their ability to come to terms with their current loss. This is not surprising, as in most cases, the loss of the child through adoption was the first major loss in the life of the mother. For adopted people, the loss of their relationship with their natural mother happened at a time when they were unable to comprehend it, but not necessarily unable to experience it. For this reason it becomes for them also, an unresolved loss.

Natural mothers are frequently offended by the terminology used by professionals in the adoption field. Natural mothers see expressions such as "the supply of babies for

119

adoption" and "the allocation of children" as commodifying their children and trivialising their pain and suffering. Professionals who are assisting natural mothers should be sensitive to these feelings and careful of the language that they employ. It is also not productive for natural mothers to be told that in being separated from their children by adoption they have "done the right thing". This attitude, in fact, invalidates their grief and supports its suppression. It is not productive for adopted people to be told how "fortunate" they are to have been adopted. This also invalidates their grief and leads to its suppression. Natural mothers often report that they have been given either no help or inappropriate advice from professionals: from doctors, psychologists and social workers. Since their families and friends often were unable to help them, they have in most cases struggled with their grief alone for many years. Adopted people also have great difficulty finding professional people who are aware of their issues.

This is one reason why it is not appropriate for those who are involved in arranging adoptions to be also involved in counselling those who are suffering the effects of past adoptions. Workers who are arranging adoptions obviously believe that adoption is a valid response to a difficult family situation. Otherwise they would not be working in that area. How then, are they going to be able to validate the grief of those who are suffering because of adoption loss?

In *Helping Women Cope with Grief*, Silverman describes the stages of grief as impact, recoil and accommodation. She describes how the role of the professional is to assist women to, '... remember the past and acknowledge and accept its influence on their futures' (Silverman, 1981, p13). She also recommends supplementing professional care with the mutual help experience. Silverman points to the incidence of depression in women and gives her opinion that the most common cause of this depression is the losses in women's lives and the way women deal with the grief which accompanies these losses (ibid p15). Many natural mothers refuse to attend adoption agencies for post-adoption trauma counselling, as these are the very agencies and the very social workers that they perceive as having caused their problem in the first place. *An adoption agency is not an appropriate place to provide post-adoption counselling to natural parents.* Many natural mothers speak very positively of the help they have received from their association with other women who have shared the same experience. Because natural mothers have violated social taboos they become stigmatised and so incur society's discomfort and disapproval (ibid p16). This corresponds with what many natural mothers describe as the feeling that they don't "fit" in society any more after losing their children through adoption. Because of this discomfort they often turn their feelings inward on themselves. The result of this is often depression, because the grief remains unresolved. Many adopted people also have this feeling of "not fitting" of always being "different" and "not belonging". This can also lead to depression and other psychological problems. Their adoption issues need to be openly acknowledged and dealt with before they can begin to feel that they are acceptable as they are.

Silverman says about the natural mother that, 'Instead of blaming society for denying her the right to mourn openly, she begins to blame herself for not being able to behave the way those around her would prefer' (Silverman, 1981, p18). Thus the natural mother repeats her perceived failure. She has failed society by breaking the taboo of sex outside of marriage and has then shattered the myth of supposed maternal dedication by giving away her baby; she then compounds her sense of failure by not being able to return to her normal life as if nothing had happened, which is what she feels is expected of her. In some studies, in fact, natural mothers have been asked how well they felt that they had adjusted to the adoption of their children. The question carries the implication that not adjusting to the loss of her child constitutes a degree of failure on the part of the mother and, therefore, may well have skewed the results.

Adopted people are expected to be grateful and often feel guilty for experiencing feelings of loss related to their adoption. Although natural mothers and adopted people do grieve and may benefit from grief counselling, their loss situation is complicated by the particular circumstances operating in adoption.

Chapter 4 The silence factor and the role of ritual

One of the simplest, yet most therapeutic ways of dealing with a loss is to talk about it to a sympathetic listener. Unfortunately, most people did not want to hear about the feelings of women who had lost children through adoption and these women did not expect people to be sympathetic. The result of this was that in most cases, the loss was never discussed. Many natural mothers of adopted children kept their loss a secret and suffered in silence. This seriously inhibited the resolution of their grief.

In *Disenfranchised Grief*, Dale Kuhn discusses the role of silence in the blocking of grief resolution and states that this often occurs, '... when a loss is unusual, or a person who has been lost ... (is) ... unknown to the family' (Kuhn, 1989, p241). He states that some people, '... feel awkward about expressing their feelings for fear that others will not understand' (ibid p241) and that this reluctance to express grief can lead to the person suffering in silence.

Kuhn expands on the issue of silence by saying that it has its roots in, '... the defenses of denial, repression, or suppression' (Kuhn, 1989, p244). Because mourners do not feel it is safe to express their grief, '... a cycle of silence ... gets established' (ibid p244). Kuhn goes on to describe how a communal silence develops which often happens because the community blames the mourner for having made a bad choice. The communal silence is often interpreted by the mourner as disapproval and this reinforces the sense of shame already felt by the mourner. The result of this silence is that the loss is not dealt with, which can lead to 'depression and other mental disorders' (ibid p245). Kuhn stresses the importance of breaking the silence in order to begin to address, '... the chaos that loss often brings - especially loss that seems atypical and is connected with guilt' (ibid p247).

In the same book, David Meagher also refers to the silence factor. He states that grief is often complicated when there is a need for concealment. The reason that the grief of the natural mother is concealed is that, 'Revelation may result in a more intense negative social response' (Meagher, 1989, p315). As a result of this concealment many natural mothers develop an anger and resentment against what they perceive to be society's abandonment of them. Shawyer puts this very succinctly when she says, 'Of course everybody knows that if she really loves the child, she will give it away and too late she discovers what 'everybody' actually knew all along but conveniently forgot to share with her - the knowledge that if she had really loved the child she would never have given it up!' (Shawyer, 1979, p5). Natural mothers feel betrayed by a society which told them to be unselfish and sign adoption consents because it would be best for their children and then made them feel ashamed of their actions afterwards.

Also in the book *Disenfranchised Grief*, Jane Nichols tackles the issues surrounding perinatal loss but also mentions adoption loss. She states that the lack of recognition of those around them of the value to them of their child sometimes leads to natural mothers holding on to their grief more tenaciously than they might have otherwise (Nichols, 1989, p122). Many women who attend support groups for natural mothers express relief at finally being able to express their feelings to someone who understands. This has been described by one natural mother as "like being in Italy and meeting the only other person who speaks English". Breaking the silence is often the first step towards grief resolution for natural mothers. The first revelation of her position is often followed by an outpouring of emotions, which have been bottled up for many years.

Joss Shawyer also published an article in the magazine *Healthright*, called *The Politics of Adoption* (Shawyer, 1985). In it she states, 'I have never heard of a case where adoption had a good effect upon the natural mother, but until women who have lost children this way speak out publicly about their suffering, society will go on unchallenged, justifying this inhumane practice' (Shawyer, 1985, p27). Shawyer's explanation for why the suffering of the natural mother has been kept hidden for so long is that, '... once her consent (and with it the baby) has been obtained she herself is of no further consequence' (ibid p27). Natural mothers were not considered to be in need of counselling after their children had been removed from them. Howe et al claim that most natural mothers "succeeded" in carrying on with their lives as though nothing had happened (Howe et al, 1992, p111) but they give no indication at all either on what research they base this claim, nor how they measure "success" in this instance. If they mean that many women have suppressed their grief and not expressed it, then I fail to see how that can be termed a "success".

Many adoptive parents profess to having been quite open with their children about their adoptive status and say that it has never been a secret. While this may be true, too often the adoption is announced once and then never discussed again. What kind of message does this send to the adopted child? They often assume from the behaviour of others that adoption is something not very pleasant, a topic not to be discussed but to be avoided. When adoptive parents do not correct visitors who, unaware of the nature of family relationships, claim to see a genetic resemblance between parents and children, the adopted child forms the impression that adoption is something unmentionable and that other people are better left in the dark. Sometimes, sadly, attempts by adopted children to discuss the situation openly are met with disappointment by adoptive parents (the "After all we've done for you, how could you?" line) and thereby discouraged.

Anthropologists have discovered a wide variety of funeral rites throughout the ages and throughout the world and it is clear that almost every culture has created a series of activities to assist the bereaved to adjust to their loss. Rituals provide the bereaved with permission to mourn. In Kenneth Doka's book *Disenfranchised Grief*, Vanderlyn Pine discusses Freud's notion that grieving allows the griever to obtain, '... a kind of "freedom" from the dead person' (Pine, 1989, p14). Many natural mothers feel that because they were not permitted to grieve they have not been able to achieve that "freedom" and so their mourning becomes chronic and unresolved. The families and friends of natural mothers are often surprised many years later to hear of the pain that they have suffered because their grief at the time was 'apparently absent'. Pine points out that this apparent absence of grief can, in fact, be a sign of acute grief which has been repressed and/or delayed (ibid p15).

Pine states that the purposes of funeral rites include; announcing the death, recognising the place which the dead person held in society, assisting the bereaved through the process of grief, delimiting the period of mourning, allowing the grievers to express their emotions publicly and allowing the members of the community to gather to support each other (Pine, 1989, p13). Pine comments on the 'pathological reactions to bereavement' caused by 'the absence of understood social expectations and acceptable rituals for mourning' (ibid p17). Often at the funeral, or the wake, friends and family members recall events in the life of the deceased person and discuss his or her personal characteristics. This provides comfort and reassurance to the bereaved. The recollection of happy events can bring a positive note to a sad occasion.

For the natural mother, there is generally no formal announcement of the birth or the adoption of her child; in fact the activity often takes place in secret. Her child is not given the opportunity to be granted a place in society as the procedure of adoption denies the child's place in the original family. Frequently no one assists the natural mother through the process of grief, as there is usually no recognition that she has suffered a loss (because she apparently "agreed" to the adoption). Because there is no ritual to delimit the period of mourning, many natural mothers describe their grief as "a life sentence". Natural mothers have no opportunity to express their grief publicly at the time of their loss, as society is embarrassed by their situation and does not grant them acceptance or permission to grieve. There is no gathering of the community around the natural mother. Instead she is often shunned and ostracised by her community. There are no happy recollections to comfort her.

There are no rituals to assist natural mothers to accept the loss of their children. Natural mothers were not even given any document to prove that they had, in fact, given birth. One of the recommendations of the Third Australian Conference on Adoption held in Adelaide in 1982 was that natural parents be provided with documentation of the fact of adoption as well as access to original birth certificates at all times. Adopted people, also, are not given copies of their original birth certificates until they become adults and may then apply for them. This is a denial of the fact that they existed as individuals prior to the adoption process. Many adopted people are not even aware that they have two birth certificates. Some adopted people, as a way of reclaiming their identity, change their names back to the original once they have their original birth certificates.

The lack of ritual is another factor that prevents the grief of the natural mother from being resolved. Many adopted people feel that because they were infants at the time of the adoption, it was something that was done without their knowledge or consent and therefore experience feelings of anger and powerlessness. There are no rituals either for them, as adults, to help them come to terms with their adoption loss.

Chapter 5 Disenfranchised grief

In his book *Disenfranchised Grief*, Kenneth Doka describes some situations in which resolution of grief does not occur, because the grief is 'disenfranchised' ie not recognised and supported by the community. He points out that, 'Most of the losses we experience are not due to physical death' (Doka, 1989, p116). Doka describes feelings of bereaved persons such as anger, guilt, sadness, depression, hopelessness and numbness (ibid p70) and states that these reactions can be complicated when grief is disenfranchised. The mourners whose grief is disenfranchised are, by virtue of this, cut off from social supports and so have few opportunities to express and resolve their feelings.

Doka describes disenfranchised grief as grief connected to a loss which cannot be openly acknowledged, publicly mourned or socially supported (Doka, 1989, p4). He expands on this description by saying that in many cases of disenfranchised grief, either the relationship is not recognised, the loss is not recognised or the griever is not recognised (ibid pp5-6).

Although Doka points out that, '... we are just becoming aware of the sense of loss that people experience in giving children up for adoption' and he acknowledges that, '... significant losses can occur even when the object of the loss remains physically alive' (Doka, 1989, p6), he does not explore further in his book the loss experienced by the natural mother. Doka does, however, mention adoption loss whenever he does a presentation on disenfranchised grief (Doka, 1998). It is obvious that the loss of a child through adoption is a loss which is not usually openly acknowledged, publicly mourned, nor socially supported.

Grief is repressed or delayed when there are no opportunities to perform the grief work. Whereas traditionally mourners would turn to their families for emotional support, because natural mothers were perceived as having brought shame on the family, that avenue of support was often closed to them. Many natural mothers report that after the loss of their child, friends and family members either avoided their company or when in their company, avoided any mention of the pregnancy or the lost child. In this way it often appeared to the natural mother that those around her were colluding with society to deny her experience and her loss. In fact those people, like the natural mother herself, had no previous experience which was comparable to this one on which to draw and were themselves at a loss as to how to react. The practice in some countries of issuing the adopted child with a new birth certificate, which states that the adoptive mother gave birth to the child, allows public denial of the existence of the natural mother and therefore of her loss.

Writing in the book *Disenfranchised Grief*, Jeffrey Kauffman states that when grief is disenfranchised, '... the bereaved may become disillusioned with and alienated from their community' (Kauffman, 1989, p29) and that this can affect one's sense of identity and belonging. Many natural mothers speak of feeling isolated and misunderstood by society in general. Natural mothers would not be surprised to hear Kauffman say that, '... loss of community that may occur as a consequence of disenfranchised grief fosters an abiding sense of loneliness and abandonment' (ibid p29). Adopted people often raise issues of their sense of identity and sense of belonging. Because they are told that, by virtue of being adopted, they are "special", "chosen" and "fortunate", their grief at the separation from their natural mother is denied, by society and often by their adoptive parents. If they try to express their feelings of grief they are often labelled "ungrateful".

Doka addresses the subject of 'elective loss' by commenting on the grief associated with abortion. Doka says that women do experience grief when they choose to terminate a pregnancy (Doka, 1989, p6). This conclusion is partly based on research, which shows the extent of bonding between the expectant mother and her unborn child. Jane Nichols, writing in *Disenfranchised Grief* about perinatal loss, states that, 'There is often an erroneous assumption that because the relationship between a newly born infant and a parent is one that is expected to exist primarily in the future, that the bonds that are joined throughout pregnancy are thus negated or nonexistent. Those who hold these attitudes are apt, then, to be unresponsive toward both the loss and the grieving parents' (Nichols, 1989, p119).

The grief of natural mothers has been disenfranchised for several reasons and in several ways. In some cases the pregnancy and birth of the child were kept totally secret because of the shame involved and so the natural mother had no choice but to conceal her grief also. In many cases, natural mothers were told by family members, by friends, by religious groups, that they were "doing the right thing". This, in fact, constitutes a denial of the legitimacy of their grief and so they often felt guilty and ashamed and thought that their grief was caused by selfishness or self-pity. The result of this denial of their feelings was often a deepening of those feelings. Many natural mothers will agree with Meagher that, '... denial does not cause feelings to disappear, in fact they grow in intensity' (Meagher, 1989, p320). Kauffman states that, '... the specific psychological phenomenon operating in disenfranchised grief is shame' (Kauffman, 1989, p25). When adopted people grow up in a family where the adoption is not referred to, they sense a feeling of shame attached to adoption. This is more intense if the adoption is actually concealed from the adopted person until they are adult. This may reflect the adoptive parents' discomfort with their infertility. It is possible that the shame felt by adoptive parents because of their infertility was actually transferred by society to unmarried expectant mothers in order to persuade them to hand over their children. Kauffman discusses the memory of past unsanctioned grief. He states that it does not evaporate over time (Kauffman, 1989, p28). Kauffman also points out that, '... when a new loss occurs, the old disenfranchisement will affect the new situation, and may enforce a repetition of the earlier inhibited grief pattern' (ibid p28). He also confirms that a new bereavement can cause a previous disenfranchised grief to emerge. Pine points out that, '... the presence of disenfranchised grief can easily complicate and compromise many other situations' (Pine, 1989, p22). Because they have often concealed their grief in order to be compliant in their adoptive families and because they have rejected intimacy because they fear abandonment, adopted people often appear cool and lacking in emotional attachment. It is important for them to get in touch with their feelings of grief and share them with others in order to be able to relate better to other people.

Shame is a word used by many natural mothers to describe their feelings at the time of their pregnancy and at the time of separation from their children. Numbers of adoptions in South Australia gradually increased from the introduction of the Adoption Act in 1925 until the introduction of the Sole Parent Pension in 1973. During this period society regarded being single and pregnant as a shameful condition. Adoption was seen as the solution to what society viewed as a problem. Through adoption it was thought that the unmarried mother would be rescued from her shameful state and the child would be rescued from the shameful condition of illegitimacy. Because of society's condemnation, single pregnant women were disempowered and manipulated by a paternalistic social structure. Many natural mothers found, however, that far from feeling rescued, they ultimately felt ashamed of having been pressured into agreeing to adoption and of having apparently acquiesced in the removal of their children. It is no wonder that they found it impossible to confront their grief as they were steeped in feelings of shame, which made them believe that their grief was not legitimate.

Many natural mothers allowed their shame to prevent them from sharing their grief with others. Kauffman states that shame can lead to a fear of abandonment (Kauffman, 1989, p26). Many natural mothers describe how for them the risk of abandonment was too great to allow them to share their grief with anyone. As a result of their fears their grief remained a secret and grew silently within them like a cancer. Natural mothers have spent many years hiding the fact that they had lost a child through adoption as they feared that they would lose the approval of friends and family members if their secret became known.

The lack of community recognition is yet another factor that blocks the resolution of adoption-related grief.

Chapter 6 Grief Resolution?

Resolution, or acceptance, is considered by many of those involved in grief counselling to be the desired outcome of mourning. Pine describes resolution of grief as the point at which the pain can be accepted and 'lived with' ie the griever, '... feels that life can continue without the one who has died' (Pine, 1989, p20). This sort of resolution is not available to natural mothers because they never know whether or not their child will return to them. In this sense they are in a position similar to those whose loved ones were missing in action during wartime. Condon points out the similarities between the two situations. He states that among the relatives of those "missing, believed dead" during wartime, 'Disabling chronic grief reactions were particularly common' (Condon, 1986, p117). When hostilities are over there are always those whose fate is uncertain and there are always those who mourn them, never knowing whether or not their loved ones will return. Resolution is therefore denied them.

Many natural mothers describe similar feelings of always wondering whether or not their child is still alive and whether or not their child will want to see them again. Natural mothers live with this uncertainty, some of them for the rest of their lives and so their grief remains unresolved and their mourning becomes chronic. Kate Inglis presented a paper at the Third Australian Adoption Conference in 1982, in which she stated that for the natural mother this, '... acceptance that appears essential to the theories of resolution of grief is ... fraught with difficulties' (Inglis, 1982, p171). The difficulty illustrated by Inglis is that of deciding what it is that the natural mother must accept.

Inglis describes the predicament of the natural mother very movingly:

Which particular thing is she to accept ... that she has a child who is lost to her but not dead; that she was responsible for its loss on the day she surrendered the legal rights and obligations of parenthood; that she lives in a world in which some mothers are rewarded and others punished for their fertility; that most people failed her, that she failed herself; that she did the right thing; that she did the wrong thing; that she grieves, that grief is not appropriate; that she is unnatural in her ability to take such a course; that she is natural in thinking of her baby before herself or conversely of thinking of herself before the baby; that she was, and still is, isolated in her experience; that her grief cannot be resolved and must somehow be lived with alone? What is she to accept to reach the tranquillity glowingly described as following acceptance in the most commonly used grief theory model. Must she also now accept another failure, ie to successfully deal with her grief? (Inglis, 1982, p171).

Because of the unique nature of the loss experienced by natural mothers, as outlined above, professionals who are entrusted with the care of these women should be aware of their particular issues and of the fact that the traditional methods of grief counselling will not be appropriate for natural mothers. Their unique experience of loss demands a unique approach. The experience of the woman who has lost a child through adoption means that her grief cannot be resolved in the same way that the grief associated with other losses can be resolved. Can it, in fact, be resolved? Should grief resolution be the goal of natural mothers? Perhaps aiming for resolution of adoption grief is an unrealistic goal and one that will only result in further feelings of failure, should it not be attained.

At the time that they were separated from their children, natural mothers were denied all of the components of grief work generally recommended by those in the field of grief counselling.

They had no rituals to assist the grief process. They were unable to achieve resolution because of the absence of finality involved in their loss. They were denied social supports. They had no opportunities to express their grief. Their grief was seriously affected by their feelings of guilt and shame. Can the mistakes of the past be somehow undone? Can natural mothers somehow experience at a later time the components of grief, which were missing from their lives at the time of their loss?

The first and most important factor for natural mothers is to break the silence that has crippled them emotionally since the loss of their children. The first step in confronting their grief is to share it with someone. In most cases, there was someone close at the time of the birth, a friend or family member who knew of the loss of the child, although they may have never discussed it since it happened. The first, tentative step could be to talk to that person about the grief and pain that the natural mother has suffered over the years. Since the natural mother has probably kept her pain to herself for many years, this person will no doubt be surprised at the feelings that are being shared. If there is no such person still in the natural mother's life, then she could choose someone she feels will be sympathetic when it comes to breaking her silence. Time enough later to discuss her loss with people whose responses may be negative. My recommendation would be that this first person should not be a member of the natural mother's current family, ie not a partner or child. If her partner or subsequent children have not been told of the lost child, there will be several issues to deal with and breaking the silence may be coupled with other factors such as accusations of deceit and feelings of betrayal. If a natural mother is unable to identify a person in her life to whom she feels able to disclose her adoption loss experience and subsequent pain, then she should try to find a support group or approach a counsellor experienced in the area of adoption loss.

Many valuable and successful support groups operate for natural mothers, which are run by the mothers themselves. In spite of the fact that some social workers, like Howe et al (1992) believe that it is necessary for, 'uninvolved group leaders' to be present at support meetings in case things, 'really ... get out of hand' (Howe et al, 1992, p134), many support groups manage quite well without this regulatory influence of professionals. Their attitude implies that natural mothers not only cannot control themselves (this is evidenced by the fact that they became unmarried mothers in the first place, one assumes) but also cannot help each other without the controlling influence of professionals. The fear of things getting "out of hand" is actually a veiled way of supporting further suppression of grief. Perhaps this represents the social workers' own fear of the depth of the natural mothers' emotions. Social workers who share these views are more likely to succeed in fostering dependence rather than empowerment among natural mothers. In fact, natural mothers usually gain more from their interactions with other natural mothers than they do from their interactions with social workers. Natural mothers who attend support groups gain confidence from each other and benefit from observing each other's growth. Howe et al also believe that having counsellors present gives, 'a sense of structure and security to the participants'. In fact, natural mothers have usually been keeping their feelings under control for many years and welcome the opportunity to express them finally without constraint in a safe and accepting environment, which can be provided by the knowledge that everyone who is present has shared the same experience and there are no observers. Natural mothers also have often felt that over the years they were being controlled and manipulated by others to conform to their agenda and so they are often very resistant to being under the control of social workers yet again. There can be a place for both, but, in general, support groups are more successful with only natural mothers present and social workers are more successful in one-to-one counselling.

For most women, the relief of breaking the silence is cathartic. It is very empowering and brings with it a flood of relief. Living with such a secret constitutes a huge mental and emotional strain and the natural mother who has become used to living this way will feel a great weight lifted from her shoulders. Adopted people also need to find someone who will recognise and understand their grief and loss issues and will provide them with a supportive environment in which to express their true feelings and address their issues.

In order to create some kind of ritual to represent the separation of mother and child, to replace the ritual that was absent at the time of the event, the first step could be to obtain a copy of the original birth certificate. The natural mother needs to know that she is entitled to have this document because it represents her experience of giving birth. It verifies what society has denied, that the adopted child is indeed her child. When she signed the adoption consent form, she lost her right to be the legal parent of that child. She did not give up the right to love her child, to care about her child's future and to have a relationship with her child.

For the adopted person, having their original birth certificate in their possession confirms for them that they did exist prior to the adoption and gives a sense of reality to that existence. Obtaining their original birth certificate can be the first step in understanding who they are and in uniting the two aspects of their identity.

In most cases the natural mother never expressed her feelings about her child because of the attitudes of those around her. For some women writing a letter to those who pressured her into giving away her child or writing a letter to her lost child will be useful, whether or not the letters are ever delivered. Some adopted people choose to write a letter to either one or both of their natural parents, expressing their feelings. For some, simply reliving the experience by sharing it with someone else will be helpful. Other ways of replacing the ritual, which was lacking at the crucial time of the separation, could be created.

It was the attitudes of those around them that led to the grief of natural mothers being disenfranchised. It is simply not possible to go back in time and change those attitudes. Natural mothers may find, however, that with the passage of time and the changes that have occurred in society, the attitudes of people to adoption loss have changed and softened with the years. In order for this to happen, adoption issues have to come out of hiding and be discussed openly and sympathetically in the community. The time for secrecy is over. Secrecy has been damaging to all of the parties to adoption. The legislators who sanctioned adoptions, the professionals who enacted adoption legislation, the adopters, the parents, family members and friends who supported the notion that the natural mother should not parent her baby; all have to live with the results of their actions. Many now defend their actions by saying that they knew no better at the time. The crucial point now is that we as a society acknowledge the damage that has been done and validate the experiences of those whose lives have been affected by adoption. Natural mothers need to be given permission to grieve and this can only be achieved by educating the general public to their sufferings and difficulties in order that more enlightened attitudes can prevail and society can provide the emotional support needed to allow natural mothers to address their grief issues openly. Increased community awareness of adoption issues will also allow adopted people to address their losses without fear of criticism.

Shawyer believes that the grief of the natural mother remains unresolved until she meets her lost child again (Shawyer, 1985, p27). Many natural mothers respect this opinion, but stress that meeting their child is only one of the steps on their journey towards resolution, not the end of the road. Winkler and van Keppel pointed out (before changes were made to Australian adoption legislation) that, '... the current practices of altering birth certificates and maintaining closed records seem to perpetuate the unresolvable grief experienced by many relinquishing mothers' (Winkler & van Keppel, 1982, p178). In spite of the difficulties regarding access to information, many natural mothers do meet their children again and begin to confront and resolve their grief.

At the Sixth Australian Conference on Adoption, Sarah Berryman, Senior Manager of the Post-Adoption Resource Centre (PARC) in New South Wales, reported on research undertaken at the centre into adoption reunions and their effects on people's lives. The researchers interviewed eighty-one people who had used the centre to mediate on their behalf. They found that a majority of 'searchers' and, interestingly, an even larger majority of 'found' people described the reunion relationship in entirely positive or in largely positive ways and that although 59% of the found people reported that they would not have searched, eighty of the eighty-one people interviewed had no regrets about the reunion (Berryman, 1997, p306). Personally, I have never known anyone whose life has been affected by adoption and who has been involved in a reunion with a lost family member to have regretted the fact that the reunion had taken place; not one person has ever expressed that feeling to me.

There is no doubt that contact between family members who have been separated by adoption is a very important contributing factor to the resolution of their grief. For those natural mothers and adopted people who never experience a reunion, however, there are ways of confronting and easing their pain. Some are able to express their feelings in art or literature. Some manage their pain by sharing it with others.

Chapter 7 Reunion and natural mothers

Having access to the adoption records of their adult children is not an unusual request for natural mothers. After all, when they signed the adoption consent, they gave up the right to parent their children. Parental rights and responsibilities end when the child legally becomes an adult; in most countries now this occurs at the age of eighteen. *The legislation that terminated their parental rights should have no effect once the child in question is officially an adult.* Parents who raise their own natural children are unable to make decisions for them once they reach the age of legal adulthood. The state should be no different; the state also should have no right to restrict information on behalf of people who are legally adults. A natural mother who wishes to contact her adult child is one adult relating to another adult. There is no other situation in which an adult can be prevented from knowing the identity or whereabouts of another adult when no law has been broken and there is no proven risk or danger involved. There is no justification for denying natural mothers information regarding the current identities and whereabouts of their adult children, just because they were prevented from raising those children to adulthood. Natural mothers, however, often do not receive support from the community when they wish to find their lost children. As Shawyer says, 'If she should try to trace the child ... she is cruelly reminded that she has served her function and that really society couldn't care less what happens to her now' (Shawyer, 1979, p5).

There have been changes to adoption laws in recent years in many Australian states. South Australia led the way in 1988 by being the first Australian state to give natural mothers and adopted adults equal rights to access information about the adoption. This move was consistent with South Australia's long-standing commitment to women's rights. South Australia was the first state to give women the right to vote and the right to stand for Parliament in 1894. The Adoption Act (1988), South Australia, allows for the release of adoption information under certain conditions. Firstly, no information will be released until an adopted person reaches the age of eighteen, unless consent is given by both sets of parents. Once the adopted person has reached the age of eighteen, that person, or, with their permission, their children, can obtain information related to the adoption, including the identities of the natural parents. At that time also, the natural parents, or, with their permission, their children, can obtain information related to the adoption, including the new identity of the adopted person. For adoptions that took place before 1988, however, the release of this information is not a legal right, unfortunately, and can be prevented by the parties involved.

As a result of the availability of adoption information, many family members who have been separated by adoption are able to be reunited. These changes came about because of demand and lobbying by those whose lives had been affected by adoption. Natural parents and adopted people were angry at being denied information about themselves and their family members. The changes to the Adoption Act reflected a change in community perceptions about adoption. Adoption is no longer viewed as a one-off event that is completed with the court order. There is now more recognition that it is a healthy emotional reaction for adopted people to seek contact with their natural families and for natural parents to wish to know the children from whom they have been separated. Sadly, other states and other countries are even less liberal with regard to access to adoption information.

There have also been changes in recent years to adoption legislation in the United Kingdom. In Scotland, adopted people have had access to their original birth certificates, at the age of seventeen, since adoption legislation came into effect in 1930. In England and Wales, adopted people have only had access to their original birth certificates since 1975. In neither country, sadly, do brothers and sisters of adopted people have any right to information about their lost siblings. Natural parents in the United Kingdom also have no legal right to access information about their adult adopted children. In contrast, I, and many others in the United Kingdom, have spent many happy hours researching my family history and have had access to records of my ancestors for the past two hundred and fifty years. I have read records of many births, marriages and deaths, yet information about the adoption of my own son is not available to me.

There is no reason why adoption information should be any different from other official records. Adoption is a legal arrangement like a marriage; there is no excuse for keeping it a secret. In Finland, for example, adoption information has always been available to anyone who requests it. There is no evidence that this has destroyed the fabric of Finnish society. I seriously hope that one day, in the not too distant future, Scottish legislators will recognise and understand the issues of parents who have lost children through adoption, as other countries have done and change the legislation to allow fair and equal access to adoption information.

I encourage every natural mother to search for her child, without reservation. The search itself is empowering as it validates her identity as the mother of her child and allows her to declare that she cares about her child. One of the barriers to grief resolution for natural mothers is the lack of finality, their total ignorance of what became of their children. Knowing the truth and dealing with it is always healthier than living with fantasy and fear. By finding their lost children, natural mothers are giving those children a great opportunity - the opportunity to know not only their mothers, but also their families and their history. This can only lead to adopted people knowing themselves even better.

When an adoption has taken place, there are two families, the natural family and the adoptive family, who are living with loss and ignorance. It is my belief and the belief of many others with experience of adoption, that a reunion between the adopted child and members of his or her natural family is to the benefit of all. For adopted people as well as natural mothers it is emotionally healthier to confront the truth than to live a half-life of fantasy or fear. Reality is always therapeutic.

Unfortunately, there is often the unwritten assumption, in books written by academics about natural mothers, that mothers should not search for their lost children and that if they do, it is something for which they should apologise. This is an insult to women who have lost children through adoption. Many women do not actively search for their children as they have been told that they have no right to search. Many do not know whether or not the law allows them to search. Many feel an obligation "not to intrude" in their lost child's current life. What I should like to say to every natural mother is, you cannot be an intruder in your child's life because you have always been there. You have always been present in your child and so you have always been present in your child's life. You have simply been waiting to be acknowledged. Offering an invitation to an adult person is not an intrusion. If it were, no one would ever make new friends and no one would ever be invited to go anywhere. An offer is· made and, in response, a choice is made.

Many people speak ignorantly of family members who have been separated by adoption as being "strangers" to each other. This is typical of the denial that surrounds adoption and of the attempts by many to attach negative connotations to adoption reunions. The relationship between those who are closely related and those who are genuinely strangers is quite different. Strangers do not search for similarities, in their physical appearances, in their personalities, in their life events, because they know that none exist.

Many natural mothers have lived with low self-esteem since giving up their children and it is difficult for them to become assertive in this matter and take the initiative and search for their children. Natural mothers have spent such a large part of their lives apologising, it is difficult for them to stop. They apologised for having sex before they were married, they apologised for getting pregnant, they apologised for giving away their children and they apologised for not being able to forget their children. There is no need to apologise to anyone for wanting to find your lost child. It is a perfectly legitimate activity. How else are they ever going to know that their mothers love them? Some fear that their child may not know of the adoption. This is not a reason not to find them. If adoptive parents have chosen to deceive your child, then they know from the outset that they risk being exposed one day and that this exposure can only harm their relationship with their adopted child. There is nothing to be gained by supporting this cruel deception. You can only help your children by releasing them from a web of lies.

Adopted people sometimes do not search as they think that the searching should be left up to their natural mother. In some cases this leads to a stand-off where each party is waiting for the other to make the first move. I encourage adopted people also, without reservation, to search for their natural mothers. Some natural mothers and adopted people are afraid to make contact with the other party for fear of somehow ruining their life. My response to that is, their life has already been permanently affected by adoption, addressing those issues can only be to their benefit. People will only address their issues, however, when they are ready. Because of the lack of community support and understanding for adoption grief, many people, natural mothers and adopted people alike, have suppressed their feelings. It takes time and effort to get in touch with those feelings again. Be patient. Do not lose hope.

Unfortunately, some who write about adoption insist on describing reunions in terms of "success" and "failure". I feel that this sort of terminology is inaccurate and unproductive. Of course, it is not always easy to be reunited with a family member after a long separation and careful preparation is advised. I strongly recommend to people preparing for a reunion that they read, talk and think a great deal before the event. It is particularly useful to talk to people who have already experienced a reunion. As Lifton says of the adopted person and natural mother, 'The separation, unresolved grief, and secrecy have traumatized them both' (Lifton, 1994, p147). This must be remembered. Family members who have been separated want to know each other. If they have undertaken some preparation before contact with the other party, hopefully they will understand that many people have been badly damaged emotionally by adoption. Many lies have been told and many feelings have been suppressed. Healing the pain is a long, slow process and it is impossible to know before contact what stage the other person has reached in that process. Some are not at a place in their lives where they are able even to start the process of healing and are not ready for contact. This is another example of the damage that has been caused by adoption, but patience and understanding will hopefully pay off in the long run. You cannot expect to undo the damage of a lifetime overnight. After all, there are tensions and differences in families that have always lived together. There is always the potential for disharmony when the family is coming together again after a long separation. There are also new people to meet; there are stories to tell, feelings to share and adjustments to be made. These adjustments can take time. It is wise to be prepared for any eventuality. Some natural parents are very distressed to find that their adult, adopted children are involved with substance abuse or illegal activities and will agonise over whether or not these behaviours are a result of being adopted.

If there are problems in relationships after family members who have been separated by adoption are reunited, the problems are caused by the original separation, not by the reunion. Problems will exist whether reunion takes place or not. It is adoption, not reunion, which causes the problems in the first place. It is not the truth that hurts people involved with adoption; it is the lies and ignorance that have gone before.

Sadly, few of the books written about natural mothers actually address the issue of them wishing to meet their lost children again. Some writers approach the idea as if it were an aberration. Howe et al (1992), for example, say of the natural mother who is trying to live with her loss, 'She may *even* want to meet her son or daughter' (Howe et al, 1992, p75, italics added) as if the very idea were bizarre. It is not bizarre to want to know your own child. It is perfectly normal and natural and to be expected. It is also in the best interests of everyone involved. Howe et al quote research from Deykin et al (1984) who studied 334 natural parents. Ninety-six per cent of those had considered searching for their lost children. Sixty-five per cent had actually initiated a search (Howe et al 1992, p96).

Verrier talks of the "primal wound" as being experienced by adopted people, but natural mothers are wounded also. In the introduction to her book, Verrier describes this wound as 'physical, emotional, psychological, spiritual and profound' (Verrier, 1993). Verrier goes on to say that the connection between the natural mother and child is 'mystical, mysterious, spiritual and everlasting'. It is no wonder then, that women who have been separated from their children want to know them. Unfortunately, in some countries, those who create adoption legislation do not comprehend this or prefer not to confront it. I was astounded and horrified to read in *Journey of the Adopted Self* (Lifton, 1994), that adoption records remain sealed in all but two states of the United States (Lifton, 1994, p304). It is morally insupportable that natural parents and adopted people are still not allowed access to information about each other in some parts of the world. While I believe that, to date, three more American states have since opened records to adopted people, none has so far enacted legislation to allow natural mothers access to information, in the way in which Australian states and territories have done.

Most people support the rights of adopted people to know their history, but natural mothers also have a moral right to search for their children. If a child is kidnapped, taken by force, we expect the parents to do everything in their power to find their lost child. *Our children were also taken from us by force*, not by physical force, but by the force of public opinion, which persuaded us that we should not raise our children "for their own good". No one should question the right of the natural mother of an adopted child to search for her lost child.

After losing their children, many natural mothers experienced feelings of numbness, emptiness, sadness, a sense of unreality and a sense of loss, among others. At the time they felt inadequate for feeling so bad. They thought that they should be "getting over it" and "getting on with their lives" and "putting it behind them", because that is what everyone was telling them to do. Many of them felt guilty and apologetic about their feelings and so did not share them with anyone. We understand now, many years later, that they had experienced a major emotional trauma and had suffered a major loss and that their feelings were, in fact, the normal, natural reaction to what they had experienced.

Some of them have been fortunate enough to be reunited with their lost children. People love to hear reunion stories and talk about "happy endings", as if the reunion itself solved everything and made it all right again. We know now that it does not. The reunion itself is another major emotional experience and for many natural mothers brings back the feelings of emptiness, loss and sadness that they felt when they were first separated from their children. Again, people are telling them that they should be happy and looking to the future and not the past and they are often made to feel guilty and apologetic yet again for still having those painful feelings even after they have met their children again.

Psychologists tell us that it takes from two to five years to recover from a major emotional trauma. It was difficult for natural mothers to recover from the loss of their children because their grief at the time was not recognised and therefore was not addressed. Finding their lost children again is another major emotional experience and they should not expect to emerge from it without significant emotional trauma. They need to understand, so that they can make other people understand, that it is to be expected that they will suffer emotionally after meeting their children again. They need to stop apologising for their feelings, which are just as normal and natural as the feelings they had after their children were adopted. They need to abolish the word "should" from their vocabulary when they discuss those feelings and accept that their feelings are legitimate in order that they can then address them. They should not feel guilty or inadequate because they are still suffering, even after they have found their children again. Natural mothers need just as much support after meeting their children again as they did after losing their children in the first place.

Chapter 8 Reunion and adopted people

Many professionals, psychologists and social workers, as well as many in the community, now understand that for an adopted person to search for his or her natural family and background is a healthy, legitimate response to being raised apart from them. This may not have been clear at the time that many adoptions took place. We now realise, however, that a reunion with the natural family is something that should be not only expected but also actively encouraged by adoptive parents. Lifton says, 'Healing begins when adoptees take control of their lives by making the decision to search' (Lifton, 1994, p128). Shawyer points out that, 'People who are not adopted spend money and time trekking the world in search of their ancestral heritage ... Family trees are pored over ... by people who know who they are ... We don't think that's strange or unhealthy, and yet adopted people ... mount the same intensive ... search, and are treated unsympathetically, even cruelly for their efforts' (Shawyer, 1979, p4).

Adopted people who deny and reject their natural families, on the other hand, are actually denying and rejecting themselves. When they acknowledge and embrace their origins, however, they are accepting themselves as whole people, made up of two families, the family into which they were born and they family within which they were raised. Similarly, adoptive parents who deny and reject the natural families of their adopted children are actually denying and rejecting their adopted children. If they cannot value their child's heritage, how can they say that they value their child?

Earlier this century there was a policy in effect in Australia, which resulted in Aboriginal children being forcibly removed from their families and placed either in institutions or with non-Aboriginal families. As a result of this policy, thousands of Aboriginal children grew up with no knowledge of their families, their language, their heritage or their culture. An enquiry into the outcomes of this policy for Aboriginal people resulted in the publication of the Stolen Children Report (1997). The whole of Australia mourned for the Aboriginal people on hearing of the trauma and heartache caused by this cruel policy. Much heartache has also been caused by adoption policies, which have separated children of many cultures and nationalities from their families and continue to do so, often for no other reason than that their mothers were unmarried and/or financially unsupported.

Adopted people, who have grown up with no contact with their natural families, should be encouraged to search for them and hopefully build a relationship with them. They should be supported in looking for what those of us who were not adopted take for granted; their inheritance, their history, their siblings and their forebears. Searching for their natural family should be easy for adopted people, in every possible way. It should be made easy by legislation, which recognises their situation and their identity issues. It should be made easy emotionally by a positive attitude in their adoptive families and in the community in general and by the recognition that searching for their natural family is a healthy, positive step in their development. It is cruel and ignorant for adopted people to be placed in a situation where they feel that they have to choose one family over the other. Having more people in your life who care about you can only be an advantage.

Some parents do not like to see their children grow and are resentful when they gain independence. Some parents have difficulty accepting a child's marriage, for example and force their child to choose between their loyalty to a spouse and their loyalty to parents. This will only damage any relationship they have with their child. Sometimes this is done out of fear that they will lose their closeness with the child simply because the child is growing, becoming independent and forming new, adult relationships. These parents, sadly, do not really wish their children to grow and develop, do not understand that this is the aim of parenthood and by their actions are actually trying to retard this growth and stifle this development. Adoptive parents who force their adopted children to choose between their affection for their natural family and their affection for their adoptive family are likewise trying to limit the number and type of warm, caring relationships their child will have. Parents who genuinely have the best interests of their child at heart would obviously never behave in this way. It can be heartbreaking for natural mothers to finally find their lost children only to discover that they have been raised by adoptive parents who have selfishly, either overtly or covertly, discouraged their children from connecting with their origins. Lifton talks about the lack of understanding among adoptive parents and in the community of the desire that adopted people have to communicate with their natural mothers. She says, 'Those who know their mothers cannot imagine what it is like not to know the woman who brought you into the world' (Lifton, 1994, p13). Adopted people who search for their natural families are a credit to the way their adoptive parents have raised them and I am sure that many adoptive parents are proud of their adopted children who have built relationships with their natural families.

Because of the fear of their adoptive parents' reactions, however, some adopted people postpone the search for their natural families until after the deaths of their adoptive parents. Far from showing respect for their adoptive parents, these adopted people are actually insulting them as they are assuming that their adoptive parents would not be happy for them to find wholeness and healing. If they postpone the search for their natural families until after the deaths of their adoptive parents, adopted people are denying their adoptive parents the opportunity to share that important experience with them. Many times, when adopted people have postponed their search for this reason, they have found that they have left it too late and that their natural parents are dead also. A sad example of this is the story of Ingrid

Pedersen, the half-sister of singer/songwriter John Lennon. Ms Pedersen was born four years after her famous brother and was separated from the family through adoption. John Lennon learned of her existence in 1964 and spent the next sixteen years, until his untimely death, desperately trying to find her. Under English adoption legislation, however, he had no legal right to information about his sister and so he was not successful. Ms Pedersen chose to wait until the death of her adoptive mother in 1998 to begin her search for her family of origin. By this time, not only was her natural mother already dead, but her half-brother also.

Adopted people who search for their natural mothers should do so with an open mind and with a genuine willingness to accept the outcome. Some adopted people find that their natural mothers have suffered greatly from having lost them. They may then mistakenly assume that, by being adopted, they have been spared the difficulties of living with a mother who went on to experience such trauma, not realising that it could well have been the loss of her child which had led to her suffering. Some mothers have even been known to commit suicide before being able to be reunited with their children. This is a particularly sad circumstance, as it is possible that had they been reunited with their children, the suicide may well not have taken place.

Robert Dessaix is an adopted person and the author of a book entitled *A Mother's Disgrace* (Dessaix, 1994). Dessaix is also a successful broadcaster and has written several books on other topics, which have been highly praised. *A Mother's Disgrace* is an absorbing and moving account of his fascination with his origins and his search for his natural family. Dessaix was born in 1944 in Melbourne, adopted as an infant and raised as an only child. He knew from an early age that his natural mother's surname was Dessaix and wove fantasies of noble ancestors. He was raised with the surname of Jones but reverted to using the name of Dessaix after the death of his adoptive parents. His book is not a linear account, but a swirl of events and connections, which sometimes feels like a literary "join-the-dots". His story includes his interest in all things Russian, his growing awareness of his sexuality, travel to interesting and exotic spots and the search for his origins.

Dessaix describes how when he was very young, he created in his mind a 'parallel world' in order to give himself a history that he 'had some control over' (Dessaix, 1994, p33). This is a common thread in the narratives of adopted people. Because they feel that the adoption took place without their knowledge or consent, they grow up with a feeling of powerlessness over their own fate. Lifton says of adopted people, for example, 'Much of their imagery is not centred in the adoptive family ... but rather in fantasy and imagination' (Lifton, 1994, p64). Dessaix tells how, when he was still a child, his adoptive father learned French, in order to be able to converse with him in that language and cites this as an example of his father's 'generosity of spirit' (Dessaix, 1994, p34). Of his adoptive mother, Dessaix says that she loved him, '... as a kind of exotic plant she'd promised faithfully to tend' (ibid p40). His mother had had a nervous breakdown before they adopted him and he was always afraid that if, '... (he) were not very good, it might happen again' (ibid p42).

Finally, as an adult, Dessaix met, in a strange coincidence, a woman who shared exactly the same name as his natural mother, Yvonne Dessaix. He calls her "Yvonne-not-my-mother". She did lead him, however, to the woman who was his natural mother. Dessaix makes it clear that the reason he decided to try to locate his natural mother was not unhappiness. He says, 'I'd never have taken the step I next took if I'd been unhappy' (Dessaix, 1994, p92). He describes himself at the time as being content with his life and says that he, '... would not have contacted her if (he) had not been content' (ibid p92). Many adopted people also search for their natural families at a time of contentment. It is quite wrong of people to assume that the search necessarily represents some sort of crisis in the adopted person's life.

Dessaix made the contact with his natural mother through the other Yvonne Dessaix who forwarded a letter from him. After reading the letter, his mother decided to call him at work, but he missed this momentous telephone call as he was in the toilet when the call came. A few days later she wrote to him, and he rang her. He describes their first conversation over the telephone as taking place 'tentatively, shyly, happily' (Dessaix, 1994, p95). They then arranged to meet.

As he walked towards her, he says his mother 'smiled a smile of boundless hurt and happiness' and that they both wanted to 'say nothing and everything all at once' (Dessaix, 1994, p96). Dessaix's mother tells him how she was afraid he would feel bitter, because she had 'abandoned' him. He is confused. He considers her 'blameless'. Dessaix refers frequently in the book to his difficulties with the fact that his mother had been raised with, and accepted unquestioningly, a value system, which was quite foreign to him. He found it hard to understand her notion that she had acted immorally by being sexually active outside of marriage. He therefore found it difficult to accept her feelings of shame connected to his birth. Between the time he was born in 1944 and the time he was reunited with his mother, in 1989, there had been a huge shift in what was considered socially and morally acceptable behaviour. He finds it hard to comprehend the degree of shame and disgrace attached to his mother's behaviour and seems surprised by the fact that his existence was never ('never ... ever, under any circumstances') referred to within the family for forty-six years, until his natural mother told his grandmother that they had had contact (ibid p89). He describes the lines of guilt and blame that he found to be 'so insidious, so intricate, someone of my generation can barely disentangle them' (ibid p113).

At the end of their first meeting Dessaix describes his feelings; '... a rush of affection, of thankfulness to this woman for being what she was, of completeness at last - no, not completeness, but completion, of weaving two parts together to make a whole' (Dessaix, 1994, p99). He says that he and his mother started their new relationship together, '... with deep, generous liking and thankfulness that the silence had been broken' (ibid p99). As their relationship develops, his mother tells him that her sense of grief 'never goes away' (ibid p114) and he grows to have a deeper understanding of the impact on her life of having been pressured by her family to give him up for adoption.

This understanding leads him to profess, '... a regret I can scarcely measure for what happened to Yvonne' (ibid p177).

David Leitch is a well-known journalist and also an adopted person. He was born in England in 1937. When he was six years old he was told that he was adopted. In 1973, he wrote a book entitled *God Stand up for Bastards*, in the hope that his natural mother would read it and contact him. She did. In 1984, he wrote another book entitled, *Family Secrets* in the hope that his half-sister, who had been lost to the family through adoption, would read it and contact him. I wonder if she did.

In *Family Secrets*, he describes how he and his half-sister were, '... both whisked away from our parents within days of our birth, the intention being to sever us from our roots for evermore' and goes on to describe the experience for him as a 'lonely and unnatural' one (Leitch, 1984, p3). Leitch expresses his anger at the legislation in England, which prevents his sister and him from tracing their half-sister. He says that his family is, '... trapped in a bureaucratic stalemate' (ibid p5). Leitch wonders whether or not his half-sister, like him, has reacted by, '... searching for a route back that would connect her adult life to her lost origins' (ibid p3).

Leitch's experience of adoption was an unusual one and its true nature only became clear to him after the deaths of his adoptive parents, Ivy and David Leitch. It was then that he discovered that not only were they never married, but that they had, in fact, never adopted him. His upbringing was actually the result of an informal fostering arrangement. Leitch grew up believing that he had been adopted, but obeying his adoptive parents' instruction never to reveal this to anyone. Leitch describes in *Family Secrets* how he felt when his adoptive mother told him about his origins and how he always knew that he would find his natural parents again, 'if it took a lifetime' (Leitch, 1984, p16). He was assured by his adoptive mother that his natural parents were, 'no damn good' and 'didn't want him' (ibid p131). Leitch's reaction to the news that he had another mother was a great feeling of sadness and pain. His very perceptive response to his adoptive mother was, "That's tough on me" (ibid p16); Ivy interpreted his plaintive, honest comment as an indication of his ingratitude. He says of that moment, 'And through the pain I could remember another earlier pain, something so terrible that I knew I would die if I ever had to feel it again' (ibid p15). He knew better than to discuss this any further with his adoptive mother, however, as she 'lived on a perilous edge of hysteria' (ibid p16) and he realised that if he persisted in discussing the hoped-for return of his natural parents, it may 'send her screaming over the abyss' (ibid p161).

Leitch describes his adoptive parents' marriage as a series of 'screaming exchanges ... near homicidal attacks ... (and) ... suicide attempts' (Leitch, 1984, p153). After the death of his adoptive father in 1957, however, his adoptive mother insisted to everyone that she and her late husband had 'never had a cross word' (ibid p157). It was only after his adoptive mother's death in 1972 that Leitch discovered that not only were his adoptive parents not married, but that his natural parents, Truda and Jack Griffith, were married. They had married, in 1937, because Truda was pregnant, then had both lost their jobs and when their first child was born, felt that they were unable to provide for him. They had found what they thought was a secure, respectable, happily married couple and asked them to look after him. Truda wrote several letters inquiring about her child's welfare. David and Ivy Leitch, however, realised that being unmarried (Ivy had been married before and had not obtained a divorce), they would never be allowed to legally adopt this child, or any other child and so they simply moved to a new area so that when Truda tried to visit her son she found that they had moved and had left no forwarding address. They virtually kidnapped him, thereby making the arrangement permanent, regardless of how Truda and Jack might feel.

In 1974, a year after *God Stand up for Bastards* was published, Leitch received a letter from Truda, his natural mother. Truda was very tentative and anxious about the possible outcomes of having contact with her son. When he received her first letter, Leitch, '... felt very loving and protective' (Leitch, 1984, p33) and wanted to reassure her that, '... (b)lame was the last thing on (his) mind' (ibid p33). He also realised from her letter that,

'... she didn't want to hear that what she had done for the best, according to her lights, had worked out anything less than ideally' (ibid p33). Leitch was very grateful to her for writing to him. Leitch was aware that, between his natural mother and himself, '... something had been retained from ... before the baby had been whisked away and turned into a new human entity called David Leitch' (ibid p43).

Leitch and Truda met in June 1974. Of that meeting he says, 'Our eyes met: recognition was total, instantaneous' (Leitch, 1984, p44). He describes how initially he, '... stood grinning at her, feeling weightless and dizzy' and how as the afternoon passed, he, '... watched her with growing affection and amusement' (ibid p45). Truda told him how she had gone to her local library and obtained his book and how as she was walking out, she looked at the inside cover and saw his baby photograph and fainted with shock when she realised that he was her child. Truda was ill for several days after this event.

During that first meeting Truda told her son about his natural father, Jack Griffith. Truda and Jack had separated in 1949. Truda also confirmed that Jack was already dead and showed her son a photograph of his full sister, Margaret, who was born in 1942. Truda was never able to bring herself to tell Margaret about David and so he did not meet her until after Truda's death. Truda also told stories of her own family and showed her son photographs of his grandfather and great-grandfather. Over the next seven years, they exchanged letters and telephone calls and the relationship grew and developed. Overall, Leitch was delighted to have met his natural mother again, although he felt some disappointment at her apparent lack of maternal feelings. He was surprised, however, at her emotional reaction to the birth of his son. When Truda saw her grandson, Luke, for the first time, in 1976, she sobbed uncontrollably (ibid p87). Leitch was aware that the loss of her children had had a long-term impact on Truda. He understood that, 'For a woman to give up her children voluntarily put a barrier between herself and the herd' (ibid p233).

In 1981 Leitch received a telephone call from his sister Margaret to tell him that Truda had died. Margaret had no idea who he was, but had found his name in her mother's address book. Leitch explained to her that he was her brother. When she recovered from the shock, she invited him to the funeral. At her funeral, Leitch thought about Truda's '... qualities of endurance and the refusal to be vanquished' and felt 'heart-rendingly sad' (Leitch, 1984, p185). His relationship with Margaret grew and Margaret confided in him that she thought that they had another sister. Sure enough, they found out that Truda did have another daughter and *Family Secrets* was written in an attempt to find her.

As Leitch reflects on the impact the reunion with his natural family has had on his life, he writes about how he, '... managed to reach an emotional peace with (his) natural mother' (Leitch, 1984, p235), although he was very aware that from his point of view, the supposed advantages that Truda thought that she was giving him, '... won't ever count as much as the losses, the childhood emptiness of knowing your parents have gone away and won't be coming back no matter how much noise you make to remind them you're waiting' (ibid p238).

The feelings expressed by these two authors are common among adopted people. The desire to connect with the family of origin is often very strong and the feeling of peace and wholeness, which is achieved by the reunion, is very powerful. There is still much that could be learned about the effects of adoption on the lives of adopted people. Accounts such as these have made a significant contribution to the understanding in the community of the benefits to adopted people of connecting with their original families.

Chapter 9 Reunion and adoptive parents

No one owns a child. Our children are on loan to us. We nurture them and allow them to grow up in a safe environment until they reach adulthood. Many of those who adopted did so in a climate of misunderstanding and had unrealistic expectations. Some people were misled into adopting children for reasons that we now realise are quite inappropriate. For example, some people thought that adopting someone else's child would somehow "cure" them of being infertile. Others allowed themselves to think that the children they were adopting were unloved and unwanted and that they were doing the children, and society, a favour by providing them with a home and a family. We now know that adoption is not a cure for infertility, that infertility is a lifelong condition to which people have to adjust, regardless of whether or not children are adopted. We also know, because natural mothers have spoken out, that in most cases the children who were adopted were very much loved, but their mothers were persuaded that they were not in a position to provide them with the kind of lifestyle that they deserved.

Many adoptive parents also are now aware of the advantages to their adopted children of having contact with their natural families. Adoptions took place generally because the natural parents of the child were persuaded that their child would receive better care and have better opportunities to achieve their full potential with parents who were married, mature and financially secure. Natural parents gave up their children because they did not want them to be disadvantaged. They then spent their lives hoping that the adoptive parents of their children had done everything possible to help them to achieve their full potential. All parents have an obligation to their children to provide the best possible environment in which they can grow and develop. It is my belief that adopted people cannot grow and develop to their full potential without a connection with their history and heritage. Adopted people who are unaware of their background are disadvantaged because half of their history is missing. Adoptive parents who genuinely want the best for their adopted children, then, will take an active role in building the relationships between the adopted children and the members of their natural families. To do otherwise is to fail in their duty of care as parents.

Some adoptive parents say that when they adopted they expected never to hear from the natural parents of the child again. They complain that changes to legislation, which have made adoption information available, are unfair. Regardless of legislation, many family members separated by adoption have been able to find each other over the years and whether or not adoption information is available as a legal right, it has always been a moral right. Because adoption information has not always been considered to be a legal right, this does not excuse efforts being made by adoptive parents, or anyone else, to keep family members apart. In fact, governments are always changing rules, especially when society becomes aware of inequities. Rules are often changed because the people affected by them complain about their unfairness. Forty years ago, female teachers who married were forced to resign from their positions. Male teachers who married were not, of course. Public opinion and increased awareness of the issues forced a change to that unfair rule. There are few certainties in life. Some changes we have to learn to live with, especially when they are changes for the better. Unrealistic assurances from social workers do not make lying and hiding the right thing to do.

Many natural mothers are very hurt by the fact that their children's adoptive parents are not supportive of contact with their natural families. Natural mothers feel that they proved their love for their children by putting the needs of their children before their own. It often makes them angry to hear that adoptive parents selfishly try to prevent their children from achieving their full potential by exploring their origins. Natural parents were told that they should show their love for their children by allowing them to be adopted. Surely it is not too much to ask of adoptive parents that they put jealousy and possessiveness aside and show their love for their adopted children by supporting and assisting them to get in touch with their relatives. Anecdotal evidence suggests that adoptive mothers who have also given birth are more understanding of the connection between their adopted children and their natural families than those who have not.

Adoptive parents who are concerned about whether or not they will be able to support their adopted children through contact with their natural families could be assisted by reading the booklet entitled, *Thoughts to Consider for Newly-Searching Adoptees*, printed by Concerned United Birthparents (CUB, 1997) in the USA. In this booklet, Carole Anderson points out that, 'There are some adoptive parents who never grow past their desire to deny infertility, to deny that they did not create their children. There are people who remain so focussed on their own need to be parents that they cannot see past it to respond to their children's needs' (Anderson, 1997, p5). Anderson goes on to say, 'It is never a child's fault when a parent refuses to grow', (ibid p6). Anderson compares these adoptive parents with enlightened, caring adoptive parents who support their children's search for their origins. She says of them, 'These are real parents and thus feel no need to prove their parenthood by denying that their children have other parents too' (ibid p6). Anderson explains that, '... developing a relationship with the birthfamily can add another dimension to an adoptee's life without diminishing other relationships' (ibid p10). Anderson goes on to say that, '... the more people are loved, the more love they have to give to all the others they care for. Real parents want their children's lives enriched with the love and support that only a variety of relationships can provide' (ibid p8). Anderson says that adopted people whose parents allow them the freedom to, '... think their own thoughts, feel their own emotions, be who they are' (ibid p9) are then, '... free to love their adoptive parents for themselves rather than because of a sense of gratitude or guilt' (ibid p9).

Joss Shawyer, in *Death by Adoption*, tells the story of Brenda, an Australian woman, living in New Zealand, who adopted two (unrelated) Maori girls, named Ann and Josie (Shawyer, 1979, Ch 16). Brenda came to realise the injustice of the girls being separated from their natural families and began to search for the girls' natural mothers when Josie was nine and Ann was twelve. Brenda believed that a reunion between her adoptive daughters and their respective natural mothers would be to the advantage of all concerned.

At the time that the book was written, Brenda had not yet found Ann's mother. Brenda did find Josie's mother, however and arranged to meet her by herself, before suggesting a meeting with Josie. Josie discovered that she had twin brothers who were full brothers. When Brenda saw Josie with her natural mother and brothers, she said, 'I felt that they belonged together and should never have been separated. I'm sure she could fit into their lives and I could accept it as being right' (Shawyer, 1979, p240). Josie's natural mother expressed the hope to Brenda that they, '... could perhaps ... do things together as families instead of splitting her from you or splitting her from me' (ibid p240). It seems that both mothers understood that they each had a close connection to Josie and that neither of them owned her. Brenda says that the experience of reuniting her adopted daughter with her natural family forced her to look things 'right in the eye' which she previously 'hadn't thought too closely about' (ibid p241). Regarding the future of this relationship, Brenda expressed the opinion that, 'things will only get better' (ibid p241). Sadly, many adoptive parents try to ignore the implications of the fact that they are raising someone else's child and choose not to confront the fact that their child has two families.

Brenda goes on to describe how she began to understand the feelings of the natural mother and came to the conclusion that adoption is 'wrong in most cases' (Shawyer, 1979, p241). Brenda describes how when she adopted her daughters she was told that the natural mothers had given them up voluntarily. This notion, of course, made it easier for her to accept the children and the adoptions. She says that at the time of the adoptions she did not want to think about the natural mother and 'the heartaches she went through' (ibid p241). Brenda says that the experience of reuniting Josie with her natural family has made her a 'better, more honest person'. She now feels 'dreadfully sorry for the mothers' (ibid p243) and believes that separating them from their children with no communication between the two is 'dreadful' and 'cruel'. Brenda says that, 'Adoptive parents who aren't honest with themselves must have lots of guilty consciences' (ibid p243). She goes on to say that, '... even if the child doesn't seem to need contact, the mother does' (ibid p243) and '... I honestly feel now that if you love a child enough, then you can't possibly lose them' (ibid p243). Brenda also says that, '... I feel now that they're borrowed, and the sooner they know their natural family the better' (ibid p243). Adoptive parents like Brenda set a wonderful example for other adoptive parents.

Another adoptive parent who was honest with himself was Pat Shannon. At a conference in Auckland in 1994 called *Adoption: Past, Present and Future*, Pat Shannon, an adoptive father and sociologist, presented a paper entitled *An Adoptive Parent Retrospective* (Conference Papers, 1994). In this paper he compares his family's experience of the adoption of his son with the long-term foster care placement of his foster daughter. Shannon tells how he and his wife adopted a child because they felt that they were doing a public service and describes their motivation with hindsight as 'incredibly precious, naive and pretentious' (ibid p64). After reading *Death by Adoption*, he says that they realised that Shawyer's book was 'fundamentally correct' and that it made them realise that they had been '... dupes of a system which forced natural parents, especially birth mothers to adopt out their children' (ibid p66). Many natural and adoptive parents now believe that they were indeed duped by a legislative system which promised natural parents a solution to what was perceived as their "problem" ie an illegitimate child and promised adoptive parents a solution to their "problem" ie infertility. Now, of course, we know that for many natural mothers their problems were only just beginning as they had a lifetime of unresolved grief to look forward to, while for many adoptive parents, raising someone else's child did not change the fact that they were, and always would be, infertile.

Once his eyes had been opened by Joss Shawyer, Pat Shannon decided, when his son was aged about ten, to search for his son's natural mother. It took four years for contact to be made. He describes how his son and his natural mother built a relationship. Although his son's natural mother is now dead, he continues to enjoy a relationship with his extended natural family and he did have the opportunity to know his mother, which would not have happened without the commitment and effort of his adoptive father.

Shannon compares this with his experience of long term (thirteen years) foster care. Throughout the period of the foster care, his foster-daughter has had constant contact with her natural parents and extended family. She did not have her identity and family history altered, as his son did, by adoption and so she had a genuine awareness of her identity and her place in the family. Shannon describes the natural mother of his foster-daughter as, '... being a constant disturbed and disturbing presence and absence' (Conference papers, 1994, p68) but still maintains that the fostering experience has been, '... a better experience than the calm, undisturbed adoption' (ibid p68). The reason he gives for this judgment is that his foster-daughter, '... is aware of her parents, had been growing up with knowledge of them and is able to live with it all' (ibid p68). Shannon goes on to say that in his opinion, '... the very worst of open relationships with all the hassle is better than the very best of closed relationships without hassle' (ibid p69). He says that contact at fourteen years was 'too late' for his son, while, if his foster-daughter's parents died unexpectedly, as did his adoptive son's natural mother, at least, '... she had the chance to know them, to grow up knowing where she came from and who she was' (ibid p70). Shannon describes the adoption process as 'a transfer of ownership' and states that, like everyone else involved, adoptive parents are also 'victims of the ... Adoption Act' (ibid p71).

Shannon also comments on the problems of infertility and the fact that, in the past, adoption was seen as a "cure" for infertility. He points out what seems obvious to us now, but was not obvious many years ago when so many adoptions were taking place, that, 'The problems of the childless cannot be avoided by taking other people's children' (*Conference Papers*, 1994, p75). In terms of future policies, Shannon is strongly in favour of supporting, not excluding, families whose children are placed in the care of others. He points out that if parents are unable to provide care for their children because of poverty, deprivation or oppression then what we should be doing is helping to alleviate those problems and, '... not take from them and their children the only thing of value they have left'. He is also in favour, on an international level, of '... supporting and assisting children in their own family, culture and nation' (ibid p77).

Many adoptive parents proudly announce that their adopted children 'have always known they are adopted', as if they have thereby fulfilled any obligation they might have to those children. We can learn a lot from the examples of these two adoptive parents, however, who not only practised honest parenting, but made extra efforts on behalf of their adopted children. They felt secure enough in their parenting roles not only to recognise what their adopted children had to gain from knowing their families of origin but also to make strenuous efforts to effect a reunion between their adopted children and their natural families.

Part Three

What does it all mean?

Adoption and Loss

Chapter 1 Reflections

I have often looked back and wondered how it all came about. Why did I get pregnant when other young women did not? I know that there were many young, single women who were more sexually active than I was. Why did I find myself pregnant with a child that I thought that I couldn't love? Was I looking for approval and admiration from men because I didn't get them from my father? Was I trying to find a man who would value me because my father didn't? Why was I so easily convinced by others to proceed with the adoption? Was it because my feelings of self-worth were not built up as I was maturing and so I could not trust my most basic feelings of love for my child? Why was I so worried about pleasing everyone else? Why was I so desperate for the approval of others? I have heard giving up a child for adoption described as a form of "self-punishment". I certainly think that there was an element of that for me. I didn't think that I deserved to be happy, or to have a child. Were the feelings of guilt and apology that I had grown up with so entrenched that I was unable to look deep inside, to get in touch with my own feelings and to be true to them? Unfortunately, my generation of young women was raised not to be assertive, but to be compliant.

Those who encouraged me to give up my child had no knowledge of his origins, as I never discussed the circumstances of his conception. I believe that they would have given me the same advice, no matter what the circumstances. Why didn't I just find a boyfriend, get engaged, get married, like everyone else did? Was I afraid of ending up in a similar situation to my mother, married to a man who was so spiteful that it seemed to me growing up that I only had to admit that something might give me pleasure for him to want to put a stop to it? But did I somehow subconsciously seek out men who would hurt me and reject me as my father had done in order to repeat the familiar pattern? My pregnancy was a result of hurt and rejection and it led to further hurt and rejection. I did finally marry a man who, on the face of things, was very different from my father. Before we were married he was gentle and caring, but after we were married I realised that he was actually very like my father in some ways. Like my father, he did not build my feelings of self-worth nor support my achievements. Like my father, he tried to destroy the things that I loved and the relationships that were important to me. Nancy Verrier said at the Sixth Australian Conference on Adoption that women who have lost children through adoption often end up in abusive relationships. Verrier said that women like me, '... feel so much guilt about surrender, they may feel they deserve abuse' (Verrier, 1997, p187).

In 1970, when my son was born, there was in place a policy, albeit an unwritten policy, to remove children from single women and hand them over to married women. This policy was in effect for many years, prior to 1970 and afterwards. This occurred in what was essentially a male-dominated society. It seemed that men could not bear the thought of a woman raising a child without a man, as this would undermine the way in which society perceived their value. To support women to raise children alone would be a threat to men's traditional role and this had to be avoided at all costs. This policy was expressed in the moral outrage that greeted news of an unmarried woman carrying a child. Traditionally, women were not expected to have sexual relationships before they were married. This expectation was prevalent in the nineteenth century, when young women were reaching puberty at the age of fifteen and marrying at the age of sixteen. By the mid-twentieth century, however, young women were reaching puberty at the age of twelve and marrying at the age of twenty-two. The expectations of their sexual behaviour, however, had not yet changed in 1969. Single women at that time were guilty of daring to go against society's expectations by having children. In fact, unmarried women did not create children, unmarried couples created children, when everyone knew that only married couples had society's permission to do so.

So entrenched was this policy, that no one questioned it; it was supported and enacted by women and men alike. Academics and social workers supported it, because they *knew* that allowing children to be raised by a woman alone would result in delinquency, churches supported it because they *knew* that it was against God's law for women to have children out of wedlock and politicians supported it with adoption legislation. Everyone *knew* that for a single woman with a child, giving the child up for adoption was "the right thing to do". It was considered a wise, unselfish act, a worthy sacrifice in the best interests of the child, a decision for which the young woman could expect a moral pat on the back. My child and I, along with many others, were casualties of this unwritten policy.

Unmarried mothers were viewed at that time, in the society of which I was a part, as a problem. Of course, problems like these are socially constructed. It was not pregnancy that was a problem but the circumstances in which the pregnancy existed. That is why all the other women in my maternity ward were being congratulated and showered with gifts when I was not. Their pregnancies had occurred within socially acceptable circumstances. In other times, in other societies, unmarried motherhood was not a problem. Over time, our society has developed a tolerance for single parenthood (except within the Mormon Church, that is, which still promotes adoption for the children of unmarried parents) and what was considered the right thing to do very soon became an awful thing to do, which is why women like me kept it a secret. When we became pregnant we were made to feel guilty because we had had sex before marriage. When we tried to make up for that, we were made to feel guilty for giving away our children. Then we had to face the dilemma of whether we gave them away unselfishly for their benefit or whether we actually gave them away selfishly to make life more comfortable for ourselves. And as time went on, we knew, above all else, that we could never find the words to explain our actions. It was easier not to try.

For many years I did not express the grief that I felt at the loss of my first child. I chose to keep it to myself because I felt ashamed and embarrassed at what I had done and did not have the confidence to share it with anyone. Now I have accepted my experience and no longer feel apologetic about it. This does not mean that I do not get angry or sad any more. I do. I am angry because I feel that I was taken in. I was duped by a society that told me that my child would be grateful for being given away and that I would get over it because it was for the best. I am sad that I was taken in and handed over my child to strangers. As time went on I realised that I had misjudged the situation. I felt used, yet again. To those who think that I should accept my fate because, after all, it was my "choice", I should like to say that I made this "choice" completely in the dark, with no knowledge at all of what its outcomes might be. I trusted those who were older and claimed to be wiser. I took a leap of faith. It was a leap in the dark. How was I to know that in front of me yawned an abyss?

I have spells where I relive the horror of my first pregnancy and the awful emptiness I felt after my child had been taken from me. I permit myself to experience those feelings when they arise and I accept that they will always be with me. I revisit those emotions on occasion and then, when the feelings are temporarily exhausted, bring myself back to the present. When I talk to people about the loss of my son, they sometimes ask me why I wanted to "rake up the past" and why didn't I "let sleeping dogs lie". When you give birth to a child, especially when that child still lives, that child does not exist in the past but in the present. Once you have given birth you are that child's mother and you will always be a mother, no matter what. Being a mother never ends; it is never in the past. There is no such thing as an "ex-mother".

Natural mothers have spent their lives apologising. We apologised for getting pregnant, but we were not the only people having sexual relationships. We apologised for giving away our babies, but we were told by everyone that it was the right thing to do for our children. We apologised for missing our children, but it was a perfectly normal reaction to our loss. Some women are still apologising for wanting to find their lost children. It is time we stopped apologising. It is right for us to search for our children. We are mothers, after all.

Now that I have explored the events surrounding the loss of my son, I see them as just that, a series of events, without any intrinsic shame or value. It has taken me many years to be able to describe these events, frankly and without apology. Because I have confronted and embraced my experience, I have robbed it of its power to shame and embarrass me. One of the main factors which allowed me to do that is the fact that Stephen has been able to accept the story of his conception, his birth and his adoption without blame or judgment. Before discussing my experience with him, I felt shame and embarrassment for twenty-one years. That is a very long time to feel guilty. When I speak to adopted people who say that they feel no need to trace their natural mothers because they do not blame them for what happened, I remind them that their natural mothers do not know that.

Chapter 2 Consequences

The loss of my first child was the first major loss in my life. The experience was such a painful and complex one that I feel that it has influenced the way I have responded to subsequent losses. Certain events dredge up the pain of that first loss, which goes very deep and which, I believe, will always be there. While I no longer feel shame, that does not mean that I do not suffer, but I no longer deny my pain and I no longer suppress it.

There have been several major losses in my life since the loss of my son. The first was the loss of my marriage. It hurt me terribly to end my marriage, as being happily married with children was my way of atoning for the "mistake" of my first child. My self-esteem was very low after the birth of my first son and being able to present a facade of a contented, conventional family was very important to me. It was one way of regaining society's approval. It was difficult to give that up and admit what I, at the time, perceived to be yet another failure. My husband blamed me, of course, for the marriage break-up and told the children that I had separated him from them because I did not want them to grow up with their father. I felt very guilty that my children were stigmatised as being part of a single parent family. I spent many years trying to make it up to them. I worked very hard to give them all the love and attention that I could, in order that they would not feel cheated by having only one parent in their life instead of two. Because of my own childhood experience, I was determined that my children

172

would be raised with warmth and encouragement. Eventually I realised that I had not failed at marriage and that I had not let my children down. If anyone had let them down then it was my husband, by refusing to work at the marriage when it was obvious that it was in serious trouble. It took me many years to shake off the burden of that guilt too. However, my children have been fortunate to receive more care and attention from me than many children receive in two parent families.

My first son was born on my brother's birthday. My brother was abroad at the time and when I did see him again, we never talked about my child. I never felt that he understood my dilemma. My brother, like my father, was a heavy drinker and he often made hurtful comments to family members when he was intoxicated. Of all those who knew, I always felt that my brother was the most likely person to tell my children about Stephen before I felt ready to tell them. After I had told my other four children about Stephen, I decided to talk to my brother and explain to him how it had all come about. I took him out to lunch and recounted my experience to him. It was such a relief to be able to share that with him finally, although I believe that he was uncomfortable with my revelations. Three weeks later he was dead, unexpectedly, at the age of forty-five, from a brain haemorrhage. I am sorry that he and Stephen were never able to meet, but I am glad that he heard about my experience.

After my mother died very suddenly and unexpectedly, in 1993, I was in a state of shock. I had never imagined my life without her. I cried every day for a year. I still cry sometimes for the loss of her sweet spirit and I know that others do too. I feel that my life has been permanently dimmed by her absence. My children adored her and she was like an extra parent to them. Moving to Australia meant that my children got to spend a lot of time with my mother and I know that they all have many cherished memories of the time that they shared with her. I feel very fortunate that I had no regrets after Mum died. I am sure that she knew how much I loved and appreciated her. I felt that there was nothing left undone and nothing left unsaid. After her death, I found among her special possessions a slip of paper. It took me a long time to identify it, as it had what appeared to be a date on it, but only the day and the month, not the year. Eventually I realised that it was the receipt from the registry office where we registered Stephen's birth. I never knew that she had kept it. In twenty-three years, she never mentioned it, even after she had met him. My mother taught me many lessons in her life. One stands out. Mum always said, "Children don't owe their parents anything. The child didn't ask to be born." Mum was right. Children do not ask to be born and they certainly do not ask to be adopted. Children raised by their natural parents do not owe them anything for their efforts. Children raised by adoptive parents do not owe them anything either. Whoever chooses to raise a child, whether their own or someone else's, owes that child the best childhood they can provide. My mother did everything she could for me throughout my life, except protect me from being hurt by my father. I still miss my mother terribly, but she lives on in my children. They have inherited her sense of adventure, her intellectual curiosity, her sense of humour, her generosity and her determination.

When my first grandchild was stillborn, in 1996, I was not only heart-broken, but also very angry. I felt that it was so unfair that I should lose my first child and then lose my first grandchild also. I felt cursed. My joy at the births of my last four children was shadowed by the pain that I felt for the loss of my first son. When my first grandchild was stillborn I knew that the births of my subsequent grandchildren would also be shadowed by the loss of my first grandchild. My first grandchild was one of twin boys. The second child died shortly after birth. Being a bereaved grandparent, I hurt for the loss of my grandchildren, but I also hurt to see the sufferings of my son and his wife. As a parent, I wanted to heal their pain, but I was very aware of my helplessness. When I knew that my first grandchild was on the way, I recalled the large, round, white shawl that I had crocheted for my first child after my marriage and I set about making one for my first grandchild, secure in the knowledge that no one would destroy it. When I knew that twins were expected, I crocheted two white shawls. My twin grandsons were wrapped together, in the shawls that I had made for them, in their tiny, white coffin. I was so angry at our loss. I so much wanted the births of all of my grandchildren to be different from the births of my children, to be completely happy events, with no tinge of sadness. It was not to be. I will never forget my two little grandsons. Happily, my son and his wife now have another son, who is strong and healthy. This beautiful little boy is very special to all of us.

After the death of my mother, I cared for my father for four years, until he died in 1997. It was not easy. He missed my mother terribly and sank into a deep depression after her death. When I told my father that my mother was dead, his first thought, as usual, was for himself. He said, "Oh no! That's the end of me", as he realised that he had lost his carer. I spent four years working very hard to keep his spirits up. He was demanding and not always appreciative. I did it because I had promised my mother that I would make sure that he was looked after if she died before he did. I felt that I owed it to her, if not to him. My father hurt me many times throughout my life. He made me feel as if I did not deserve to be in the family, even when I was forty years old and he wanted to arrange their Golden Wedding celebrations for a date when he knew that I could not be there (I had already booked my overseas trip). Throughout my tender years, my father did not nurture my spirit. He did not help me to value myself. He did not encourage me to achieve my full potential nor praise me for my achievements. Now he never will. During the four years that I cared for him, however, I came to realise that, at that stage in his life, he was just a lonely, old man. Over the four years, he slowly came to appreciate my efforts and achievements. I heard him say "Thank you" to me for the first time in my life, only after my mother died. I slowly came to understand how much he had lost and what he had missed in his life. We grudgingly began to make allowances for each other.

At his funeral, I had what I can only describe as a vision of him. He suddenly appeared before me, smiling and happy. This vision was quite incongruous, firstly because funerals are mostly sad events and secondly because my father seldom wore a cheerful expression. I had a very strong feeling that this was his true self, which had been hidden throughout most of his life. It came to me that the difficult, selfish persona that he had adopted was in some way a test, for me and perhaps for the rest of the family. Finally I felt that I saw through his mask to the real person inside. I thanked him for what he had taught me. I am glad that I did not let my bitterness prevent me from spending that four years with him and from finally seeing the part of him that he had kept hidden for so long.

All of these other losses have drawn me back to that early loss and I have relived it on each occasion. All of these losses are a part of my life. They have helped to shape me and to teach me. I have no doubt that there will be other losses in my life, but I will experience them, I will confront them and I will incorporate them into my life. Never again will I hide, deceive and feel shame. There will be no more secrets and no more lies.

When I was a child, I had a dream. My dream was to escape from the predictable, seemingly inevitable lifestyle in which I had grown up. My one goal was to have an interesting life. To achieve that I wanted to travel, gain an education and undertake interesting and challenging employment. When I discovered, in October 1969, that I was pregnant, I thought that my plan had been sabotaged. As a child in Scotland, however, I grew up with the story of King Robert the Bruce, who watched the spider trying to make a web and learned to try, try, try again and never give up. I did not give up.

In fact, I have done all of the things that I wanted to do and I have certainly achieved my goal. I am grateful to Mr Campbell, my primary school headmaster, for seeing my potential and encouraging my parents to allow me develop it. I am grateful to my mother for supporting me in attending a grammar school and I take credit for making the most of my opportunities there, in spite of feeling that I did not fit because of my working class background. My mother allowed me to go to university and I succeeded there because of my hard work, in spite of having no family support and spending my final year enduring an unplanned pregnancy. I received my Master of Arts degree (an undergraduate degree in Scotland) from the University of Edinburgh in 1970. I then moved to Bermuda, took up a teaching appointment (in spite of the fact that I had no training or experience as a teacher) and spent four very happy years working there. I married, returned to Scotland and had four planned and very much wanted children. I chose to end my marriage because I realised that no matter how badly I felt about myself, I deserved to be treated with respect and my husband seemed unwilling to do that. I then moved with my children to Australia, a totally unknown country and within three years of arriving in Australia had completed a post-graduate Diploma in Education at the University of Adelaide, bought a house and started work as a high school teacher. I then returned to study in 1995, completed a post-graduate degree in social work at Flinders University and gained employment as a social worker. Then I wrote this book. Whatever else my life has been, it has been interesting. I have had five varied and challenging careers, as a full-time mother, a high school teacher, a customer service officer, a social worker and now an author. I have travelled extensively and have produced five admirable children. When I left Renfrew as a teenager in 1967 to live in Edinburgh, I felt as if it were the other side of the world. Now I am truly on the other side of the world. I have lived in Adelaide, South Australia since 1982.

I have spent many years recently helping those whose lives have been affected by adoption. I have presented conference papers on adoption issues. I have addressed many audiences such as political groups and support groups. I regularly present workshops on adoption to student pastors at the Adelaide College of Divinity and to student social workers at Flinders University. I have had work published in the newsletters of many organisations, such as the National Association for Loss and Grief, Australian Association of Social Workers, Adoption Jigsaw and ARMS. I have been interviewed on several occasions by the media on adoption-related topics. I am now employed as Counsellor/Co-ordinator with ARMS and have counselled many people on a one-to-one basis and shared ideas with many more.

I do sometimes wonder what might have happened if I had not agreed to allow Stephen to be adopted. It is not a comfortable feeling to think that I may have benefited from giving him up. It is difficult enough to admit to having given away one's child without the suspicion that I was somehow better off because of it. When I consider my journey through life, however, I believe that I achieved my goals, not *because* of the fact that my son was adopted, but *in spite* of it.

To the people who say that they love a story with a happy ending, I should like to reiterate that the story has not always been happy and that it has not ended. My child and I were separated from each other for twenty-one years. There is nothing happy about that. In spite of the fact that I am delighted to have him as a part of my life, I still experience sadness and pain when I remember what I have lost. Those lost years can never be replaced. If I had had any idea of the pain that I was going to suffer I would certainly not have allowed myself to have been persuaded to agree to the adoption. "But", you will say, "surely the child's interests must come first? Wasn't it better for him?" There is no way of knowing whether or not it was better for him. We must deal with what we know. I do know that I raised four children alone and that they have become confident and productive adults of whom I am proud and that Stephen has now united the two parts of his identity and understands himself a lot better for knowing where he came from. Our search for each other was a search for wholeness for both of us.

As for me, raising four children single-handed did not prevent me from achieving my goal; I cannot see how raising one would have. I believe that I have "made something of myself" and I am proud of my achievements. I have used what I have experienced to learn and to grow and to help others to grow. If you are reading this and you are the secret mother of an adopted child, then what I should like to say to you is, own up, release yourself from the agony of secrecy, talk about your child, be true to yourself and to your child, own your history, find your child, lay your demons to rest and find peace. If you are afraid that others will not accept you for yourself, trust them. They may have difficulty coming to terms with it in the beginning. Give them time, they will come round. Give them the opportunity to love you for who you really are, a mother. Being yourself and being known for your whole self will open up lines of communication and deepen relationships. If it creates problems in a relationship that cannot be overcome, then you have to ask yourself how valuable was the relationship in the first place.

Chapter 3 What is adoption?

What is adoption? What does it do? Adoption is a legal transaction by which a child ceases to be the legal child of his or her natural parents and becomes instead the legal child of his or her adoptive parents, as if born to them. Adopted children are issued with a new birth certificate and their original birth certificate is no longer a legal document. Adoption permanently severs all legal, family connection between the adopted child and his or her natural family members. Once a child is adopted, the natural parents have no legal right to any information about that child and will not be told if the adoption has been terminated or if the child has died. Traditionally, adoption has operated to transfer children from the weak to the powerful, from the poor to the financially secure. While many thought that adoption was a solution to society's problems, we now know that a heavy price has been paid by those involved for what appeared at the time to be a simple answer.

In South Australia, the number of adoptions peaked in 1970-71 at 879. By 1997-98, the number of Australian-born children adopted in South Australia had dropped to just 4. Australia-wide, approximately 10,000 children were adopted in 1971-72, while only 559 were adopted in 1997-98. The reasons for this dramatic change are fairly obvious. Sex before marriage is now the norm as opposed to the exception. Attitudes to single parenthood have changed considerably over the years and it is evident that there is much more tolerance now for women raising children alone. Legal abortion is now much easier to obtain, being available virtually "on request". In 1973 the Australian federal government introduced a payment designed specifically for single parents. After this date the number of adoptions dropped dramatically, which suggests that many babies were lost to adoption principally because of financial hardship. In the last twenty years more women than ever are in paid employment and there has been a significant increase in the number of childcare places available. All of these factors combine to explain the very low numbers of adoptions taking place in South Australia at the moment. This trend is evident in the United Kingdom also.

Although there are few adoptions happening now, there is still a huge number of people whose lives have been affected by adoption. Legislation caused these problems. Legislation is created by politicians. Governments now need to own up to the damage that has occurred because of adoption legislation and to provide funding for adoption-related counselling for all those whose lives have been affected by adoption, in order that the counselling services will be available free of charge. This would constitute an acknowledgement that governments are responsible and that they are willing to accept responsibility and take steps to repair the damage.

As a result of the *Stolen Children* report, completed in 1997, which detailed the outcomes of the policy which separated Aboriginal children from their families of origin, the Australian federal government allocated $63,000,000.00 (approximately 20,000,000.00 pounds sterling) to repair the damage. This was, finally, an acknowledgement of the pain that had been caused by this villainous policy and an admission of responsibility, if not guilt. *No federal funds at all*, however, have been offered to the thousands of non-Aboriginal family members who have been separated from each other by adoption policies. Governments around the world should also take responsibility for the thousands of families that were damaged by government adoption policies and allocate funds to assist them.

Expressions such as "the adoption triangle" and "the adoption triad" are misleading as they give the impression that the only people affected by an adoption are the adopted person, the natural mother and the adoptive parents. In fact the effects are much more wide reaching. There is the natural father (often, sadly, forgotten), his parents, his subsequent partner, his subsequent children, the parents of the natural mother, her subsequent partner, her subsequent children, the adopted siblings, the adoptive grandparents, the partner of the adopted adult child, their children, to name but a few. All of these family members are affected when a child is adopted. The consequences of adoption are not only wide reaching, but also permanent. An adoption can never be undone; it can only be lived with.

Adoption was introduced, ostensibly, to provide homes for children who were unable to live with their natural families. In fact, the main criterion for being able to adopt a child was infertility. This factor, alone, makes governments' true agenda obvious. No one, surely, could claim that being infertile ensures that one is going to be a more responsible and caring parent than someone who is capable of producing their own child. In fact, in many cases, failure to come to terms with their infertility had an adverse effect on the relationship between adoptive parents and their adopted children. It is interesting, in this respect, that several studies have been conducted on the mental health of women who have lost children to adoption, but none, as far as the author is aware, on the mental health of the women who actually adopted those children. It is obvious from this policy that the hidden agenda was, in fact, to provide children for childless couples. It needs to be said clearly and emphatically that the purpose of adoption, if, indeed, it ever had any defensible purpose, was not to put smiles on the faces of adoptive parents. *Adoption is a service for needy children, not a service for needy adults.* Many adoptive parents speak of wanting to express their "thanks" for the "gift" that they have received ie someone else's child. This sort of statement is offensive to many whose children were lost through adoption for several reasons. Adopted children are not a "gift", as some seem to believe. A gift is a commodity, which is passed freely from one person to another. In most cases natural mothers did not voluntarily "give" their children away, they felt driven to abdicate the role of parent under considerable pressure. A child is not a commodity to be handed over from one person to another like a birthday present. Adopted children are real people who have been separated from their original families. Natural mothers did not give up their children for the purpose of making adoptive mothers happy and many of them do not want to hear someone "thanking" them for having suffered so much. Adoptive parents who express gratitude for the child they have "received" are saying that they are happy to have benefited from someone else's tragedy. Talking about a child as a gift takes the focus away from the fact that adoption was supposed to meet the needs of the children and emphasises instead the fact that *adoption actually met the needs of adoptive parents*. This emphasis is inappropriate. Adoptive parents who use this sort of terminology make it clear that they are happy that their needs were met by adoption.

In South Australia, as recently as 1988, in Schedule 3 (Regulation 8) of the Infertility (Medical Procedures) Regulations 1988, Prescribed Matters for Counselling, in Section 1, entitled *Counselling of a woman and her husband prior to, and for the purposes of, making a decision regarding participation in a relevant procedure*, Section 1.2 mentions, with reference to counselling infertile couples, 'The range of options/choices available to resolve their particular situation, including adoption'. Regardless of what government agencies advise about changes in policy to the effect that adoption is no longer seen as a service for infertile couples, this points to the fact that, as late as 1988, adoption was still considered as a 'resolution' for infertility. This is totally inappropriate and it is very discouraging to find this kind of statement in information for debate in the National BIOETHICS Consultative Committee's issues paper on infertility counselling, published in July, 1990. The committee does point out that a pregnancy is not a 'cure' for infertility, in the same way that an adoption is not a 'cure'. Disappointingly, however, the committee considers adoption as a 'social option' for infertile couples (ibid p22). The Overview and Summary to the issues paper, points out that, 'A consistent theme of this report is that a range of options are (sic) available for the resolution and management of infertility'. (ibid piii). Sadly, adoption is considered to be one of those options, which, according to the committee, will lead to the resolution and management of infertility. In this they are sadly misled. Adoption is not a treatment for infertility. No one has a right to have a child. Some people have children. Others do not. A person born without an arm does not expect another person to donate theirs. People without children should not expect other people to donate their children either.

An adoption is *never* a reason for celebration. Every adoption is a tragedy because it means that there has been a family breakdown. A mother and child constitute a family. When they are separated, for whatever reason, that family has broken down. How can that possibly be a matter for celebration? An adoption means that a child has been irreversibly separated from his or her mother. There are several reasons why this happens. In some cases the mother is incapable of caring for the child, but most often she is simply unaware of her rights as a mother and is swayed by society, represented by parents, social workers, doctors and ministers of religion, into parting with her child supposedly "for its own good". In many countries, tragically, there are still many adoptions that take place without the consent or even knowledge of the mother. In many cases welfare officials decide that a child would be "better off" with another family and are able to obtain a court order for a compulsory adoption. Social workers in the United Kingdom euphemistically refer to this as "freeing" the child for adoption, which means dispensing with parental consent. If anyone does not believe that this barbaric practice happens relatively easily and arbitrarily, I recommend that they watch a film called *Ladybird, Ladybird*, directed by Ken Loach, which is based on a true story. It tells of a woman in Britain who lost six children through compulsory adoptions and this happened in the early 1990s. The film is harrowing, especially the scene where the woman's new-born infant is taken by social workers, accompanied by police officers, from the maternity hospital while the mother is sedated to prevent her from holding on to her child. As recently as 1992, Howe et al stated that, in the United Kingdom, '... the number of mothers whose children are compulsorily removed and placed for adoption against their wishes is increasing' (Howe, Sawbridge & Hinings, 1992, p4). This is an appalling state of affairs and one of which the United Kingdom should be thoroughly ashamed.

In many so-called "third world" countries, from which children are adopted every year into developed countries, it is not illegal to adopt children without the knowledge or consent of their parents, but this is often done informally, sometimes by telling the mother that the child has died. In an article in a popular Australian magazine, a few years ago, a supposedly Christian, South Australian couple who adopted a disabled child from Romania, after a long battle with the immigration authorities, were interviewed. They proudly announced that they had adopted the little girl, knowing that her mother had been told that she had died. Many illegal adoption transactions of this nature have been exposed. Many children from other countries are adopted illegally and immorally without the knowledge or consent of their parents. There must be many adoptive parents who have this on their consciences.

There is currently concern in many countries over the increasing numbers of children born to single women and especially very young, single women. In Glasgow, Scotland in 1998 more than 50% of the babies born were born to unmarried couples. What is frightening is that a punitive attitude is growing towards young, unmarried women who have children. This is particularly common in the United Kingdom and the United States. Adoption is being suggested as a way of punishing young mothers and as a deterrent against future pregnancies. Adoption must no longer be used as a punishment against women and their children. Hopefully, education and awareness will prevail and people will not continue to delude themselves that adoption will be a solution. It would be more helpful to provide support to young, inexperienced mothers and teach them how to care for their children. It would also be useful to explore issues such as why are so many young, single women having children, are they making an informed choice in the matter, are they fully aware of the consequences of their actions and how can education help. It is interesting to note that in South Australia, the number of teenage mothers is gradually declining in comparison to the remainder of the female population. In 1998, births to teenage mothers in South Australia represented 18.5 out of every 1000 births, compared to 22.1 per 1000 in 1990. In the United Kingdom, however, the number of teenage mothers giving birth in 1998 was as high as 63 in every 1000.

As a social worker, I have worked with many homeless young people. Some of them are adopted, some come from step-family situations, some from families in which their natural parents do not live together and some from what appear to be traditional families with none of the aforementioned issues. All of them have feelings of rejection or abandonment by one or both of their parents. In some cases a parent has left the home and not continued to show concern for their child, in others a parent has remarried and the child perceives that the parent puts the needs of the new partner before the needs of their child and in some cases children feel that although their parents live with them, they do not value them. These feelings of rejection and abandonment usually are expressed as either depression or anger. Feelings of parental concern, acceptance and unconditional love are vital to a young person's sense of belonging and general emotional well being.

Some adoptive parents have difficulty relating emotionally to their adopted children. This may be because they are not able to see their own qualities, or those of their partner, reflected in their children in the way that parents who raise their own children do. At the 11th World Congress on In-Vitro Fertilisation, held in Sydney, Australia in May 1999, the Congress chairperson, Dr Robert Jansen, talked about parents who have children from anonymously donated eggs and sperm. He said, 'In a sense they're creating an alien in their own family, not a child that represents the features that attracted them to each other in the first place', as reported in The Australian newspaper on 15/5/99. What Dr Jansen says of children created from donated sperm and eggs is also true of adopted children. They do not exhibit and reflect either the physical features or the personality traits that originally attracted the adoptive parents to each other. It is easier to accept our children's sometimes challenging qualities when we have to admit that they inherited them from us.

Sadly, some of those whose lives have been affected by adoption feel insulted when adoption is criticised. Thousands of children were adopted, many of them in the 1960s and 1970s. Thousands of natural mothers were separated from their children. With hindsight, this seems to constitute cruelty on a massive scale. When I discussed this with one adoptive mother recently she said that she believed that, one day, we would look back at adoption and wonder how we could have done it. I told her that she did not have to wait, that people were saying that now.

I believe that my case is typical in many ways of thousands of others. I believe that those who were involved in arranging the adoption of my son, the social worker, the church leaders, my son's adoptive parents, all acted with the best of intentions. I do not believe that any of those people intended to cause suffering or harm to my child or myself. They thought that I, and others like me, had to be deterred from repeating the mistake of producing a child out of wedlock and that my child had to be protected from the outcomes of that mistake. I also acted in good faith. I was persuaded by all of those people that adoption was the right thing and was in my son's best interests. I acted in ignorance and I am very fortunate that my son understands that. The others also acted in ignorance and I understand that. I do not blame them any more than my son blames me. Criticising adoption is not the same as criticising those who have been involved in adoption. It is not about blame. I was involved in an adoption and I am not offended when adoption is criticised. I welcome an explanation of the motives behind adoption and an exploration of its future. I am concerned for everyone whose life has been affected by adoption. I hope that they will all be prepared to read, to discuss and to learn. I sincerely hope that professionals with an interest in the adoption area will also be prepared to read, to discuss and to learn, especially to learn from those with personal experience. Everyone, especially those whose lives have been affected by adoption, should join me in welcoming further exploration and explanation.

What is crucial is that we can no longer plead ignorance. Adoption has caused a huge amount of emotional damage to an enormous number of people. It can be tolerated no longer. Those who are still ignorant of the outcomes of adoption have chosen to close their ears and their minds. Ignorance is no longer an acceptable excuse. There is overwhelming evidence that adoption has been damaging, for natural mothers as well as for adopted children and it is essential for the future well being of families that we acknowledge those facts. As Shawyer said, 'Women can and must stop putting in orders for other women's babies' (Shawyer, 1985).

Chapter 4 The way ahead

When I addressed the Sixth Australian Conference on Adoption, I spoke of the rage that had driven me to write my paper. I expressed my anger at the sufferings of natural mothers in the past and at the fact that women were still suffering and would continue to suffer in the same way until legislation was passed to make adoption what it should be, a thing of the past. I will continue to be angry until there are no adoptions. People have said to me that I *shouldn't* be angry. I disagree. I am angry, but I am not bitter. Bitterness is a sign of defeat. Anger can be used productively to bring about change. Gandhi was angry. Rosa Parks was angry. Emmeline Pankhurst was angry.

There is no justification for adoption. Why do some governments persist in issuing adopted children with new birth certificates, which are a fabrication? It is offensive to natural mothers to find that both their existence and their experience are so easily obliterated with the stroke of a pen. Adopted people also object to their original details being officially erased. Lifton describes how, because of the fact that they are issued with a new birth certificate, adopted people grow up believing that their 'birth heritage is disposable' (Lifton, 1994, p50). Shawyer describes the falsification of birth records as, 'an insult to personal dignity' (Shawyer, 1979, p4).

Our moral awareness is continually growing. Policies and practices that once were acceptable are no longer tolerated.

Slavery was legal in the United States until just over a hundred years ago. Now it is abhorred. In 1999, we are appalled to think that communities once bought and sold people, uprooting them from their families and transplanting them elsewhere. To us, it is clear that slavery is ethically wrong and morally indefensible. We wonder how apparently upright, moral people, such as ministers of religion, could not only defend but practise slavery, extolling its virtues. Slavery's defenders pointed out that slaves were better off being owned by a good master, that it provided them with a home and security and rescued them from a life of disadvantage. Slaves were expected to be grateful. It took a long time for these ideas to be challenged. Now we take for granted the basic human right of freedom, the respect for human dignity that does not allow trade in human beings. Why did people buy slaves? Because they wanted them and society said that they could.

In some countries, such as Australia, adoption is still legal. In some countries it has never existed and never will. In such places, people would react with horror to the very idea of permanently changing the parenthood and genealogy of a child. Adoption's defenders describe how adoption saves children from a lifetime of disadvantage, gives them security and a good home, for which they should be grateful. Does that sound familiar? Why did people adopt children? Because they wanted them and society said that they could.

It is time for society to realise that adoption is ethically wrong and morally indefensible. The idea that adoption is socially acceptable needs to be strenuously challenged. People need to be educated to see adoption for what it is, and to abandon it, in the same way that they had to be educated to denounce slavery.

Sadly, most academics who write about adoption take it as a given and do not question its existence. Howe et al, for example, write about, '... the conditions that make adoption necessary' (Howe et al, 1992, p74). There are no conditions that make adoption necessary, because *adoption is not necessary* and it never has been necessary. Adoption was a social experiment. The tragic outcomes of this experiment make it clear that the way ahead must be a future without adoption. Robert Ludbrook, a lawyer and founding member of Jigsaw, presented an interesting paper at the Adoption and Healing Conference in New Zealand in 1997 entitled *Closing the wound*, sub-titled, *An argument for the abolition of adoption*. In it he explains why he believes that, '... adoption no longer serves any overriding social purpose which outweighs its negative aspects' (Adoption and Healing, 1997, p57). At the time of writing this book, January 2000, the New Zealand government is considering the question of whether or not to abolish adoption and replace it with a system of "legal parenthood" which would convey the rights and responsibilities of parenthood without changing the child's identity and without involving secrecy and inaccessible records. It will be very interesting to see if New Zealand has the courage to take the lead in putting an end to adoption and putting the effort into creating a more humane alternative.

Mothers grieve for the loss of their children and children grieve for the loss of their mothers. Natural mothers and adopted people deserve appropriate services to assist them to deal with their grief, but we must be very careful to distinguish between addressing the needs of those whose lives have already been affected by adoption and preventing further grief. There is no evidence, to my knowledge, that providing counselling before removing women's children from them will prevent them suffering from future grief reactions associated with the loss of those children. There is no "right" way to perform a permanent, legal separation of a mother from her child. Regardless of any counselling which occurs, these mothers will still have to deal with the fact that they have apparently voluntarily given away their children and that their children still exist and so their loss will never be final. Those mothers whose children are taken from them without their consent are still considered to be responsible, as the separation has apparently been caused by their failure to provide a safe home environment for their children. Neither is any amount of counselling for mothers at the time of separating them from their children going to help those children to come to terms with their loss. Mothers and children separated by adoption grieve because they have been separated. Extenuating factors exacerbate their grief, but the actual cause of the grief is the separation itself.

There are certainly children, sadly, who are not safe with their natural families. How are we to care for them? A safe environment needs to be found for them, preferably with members of their extended family or social circle, in a situation with which they are already familiar. Family links should be maintained at all costs. There is never any need for a permanent, legal separation of parents and children. If there are children who are genuinely not safe growing up with their original families and find themselves growing up with those to whom they are not related, their original names and identities must be maintained. There must be no more pretence and denial. These children have a right to know who they are and to whom they are related.

Adoption has traditionally been used as a punishment for the parents, although welfare agencies would not admit to this. What they fail to realise is that this separation is also a punishment for the children. Separating parents from children does not teach the parents to modify their behaviour, nor does it offer them any hope or incentive to do so. It does not teach them parenting skills; it also does not prevent the parents from having more children. If our current foster care system is not serving children well, that is no excuse to continue to have them adopted. That is a reason to improve the service we can provide to children in need. The whole system of alternative care for children needs to be redesigned with the best interests of children in mind. We need to look closely at foster care and at guardianship so that we can provide what children need, whether it is short term or long term care. Our children deserve the best care that we can provide for them. I have great admiration for those who open their homes to children in need, expecting nothing in return but the satisfaction of knowing that they have made a difference. There is a trend in many countries now towards family preservation programmes, in which efforts are made to keep families together. Hopefully, these will gradually take the place of adoption policies, which actually cause family breakdown.

There are some who say that children need the security of adoption. Children do, certainly, benefit from a feeling of security, but they do not necessarily obtain that from being adopted. In fact, it is not an adoption order that provides children with security. In many cases people adopt a child only to decide after some time that they no longer want the child. The child is then returned to the authorities, sometimes fostered, sometimes re-adopted. It is unconditional love that provides children with a feeling of security, not a piece of paper. Many children feel happy and secure living with people who are not their parents, regardless of whether they are adopted or not and, sadly, many children do not feel appreciated, nor secure, living with their natural or adoptive parents. Adoptive parents sometimes divorce and separate, they abuse and neglect their children, just as natural parents do. What children in need of care certainly do deserve is to maintain their identity and their links with their families and to grow up with honesty and openness. Our children and our families deserve the best possible service in times of crisis.

There seems to be a growing emphasis, especially in the United States, on the provision of material possessions. Young women are still being pressured into giving away their children simply because they are in a disadvantaged position (which is probably temporary) financially. This emphasis is quite inappropriate and very saddening. A sense of belonging and of being valued cannot be bought. I am sure that if a random sample of the adult population was questioned about their fondest childhood memories, very few of them would mention the amount of money that was spent on them. Children and their parents should only be separated when there is an issue of the child's safety, not ever simply because someone else is in a position to spend more money on that child.

Women must stop taking other women's children. If a woman is unable to care for her child because she lacks the skills, then we should try to teach her the skills. If a woman is temporarily in a situation that would be unsafe for her child, then by all means care for the child elsewhere, but in the meantime help the woman to get out of her dangerous situation. If poverty is the issue, then strategies need to be put in place to address the poverty. Women in trouble need support. They do not need to be made to feel even more powerless by being robbed of their children. We must stop using the *permanent* practice of adoption to solve what are often *temporary* problems. If there is a permanently unsuitable situation, for example where the mother suffers from a mental health problem which would put her child at risk, then we should arrange for the child to be cared for elsewhere, but should not abandon and punish the mother. Both mother and child will benefit from enjoying an on-going, if necessary supervised, relationship. There is no justification in such cases for changing the child's identity and pretending that the child has a different mother. If a woman wishes to have a child and is unable to, she has no right to take a child from another woman to fulfil her desire. Adoption is largely a women's issue as women are the ones who bear children. Men, unfortunately, are most often the ones who make adoption policies. Women must make their voices heard and force changes to outdated adoption policies.

There is talk now of so-called "open adoption" although there is a lot of confusion as to what this term actually means. In South Australia, for adoptions which have taken place since the Adoption Act (1988) was passed, there is no longer the ability for any of the parties involved to prevent the release of information once the adopted person has reached the age of eighteen years. That is the only way in which current adoptions are in any way "open", compared to adoptions which took place prior to 1988. There is also now the option for information to be exchanged between the natural parents and adoptive parents, while the adopted child is under the age of eighteen years, via the Department of Family and Youth Services, of course, not directly. These arrangements or "adoption plans" as they are called, are not enforceable and purely voluntary. Anecdotal evidence shows that they tend to break down after a fairly short period of time. There is, of course, no evidence as yet as to what impact this exchange of information might have on the natural mother or the adopted child in terms of grief resolution. My feeling is that there is no way to make the loss of one's child or the loss of one's mother more palatable. An adoption is an adoption, "open" or not.

Because there are very few Australian women consenting to the adoption of their children now, infertile couples in search of children in recent years have tended more and more to look overseas. Sadly, there are parts of the world where they are currently unable to support the population and the children often suffer. People are being duped now, as they were many years ago, into believing that they are providing a community service by adopting children from countries where people are less well-provided for than in most developed countries. They rush to the rescue, as they see it, instead of respecting the need for other countries to work out their own destinies in their own ways. If people in other countries are living with the problems of poverty, repression or famine, the way to alleviate those problems is not to remove their children and thus break up families and cause further suffering. Those who are concerned about these issues could be supporting ways to improve conditions for those who are suffering, not add to their suffering by taking their children from them. It may be that the social conditions, which are causing children to be separated from their families, will change gradually over time, in the same way that they have changed in Australia over the years. These changes may be delayed if the current system continues to be supported by children being adopted to other countries.

Instead of spending many thousands of dollars raising someone else's child, those who are genuinely concerned about the plight of these children could send that money to the country in question to allow the family to raise their own child in safer, more secure circumstances. Some people salve their consciences by saying that they only adopt children who have already been abandoned in orphanages and that if they were not adopted and taken out of the country, those children would never know what it is like to grow up in a family. In fact, many parents in such countries are driven to lie and say that their children are orphans because they know that that is the only way to ensure that they are fed and cared for. Even genuine orphans have extended family members. They have a community and a culture, which are valuable to them and in which they are valued. Those families and that community suffer from the loss of their precious children.

If people are genuine in their concern for these children, instead of uprooting them from their homeland, why are they not investigating the reasons why families are being pressured into placing their children in orphanages in the first place? Why are they not trying to solve the problem at its roots instead of simply continuing to rob that country of its future generation? Removing a country's children can only be destructive to that country's future. Behaving this way is like trying to blow out a gas fire with little puffs of air, instead of simply turning off the gas. If the plight of the children is their real concern, instead of taking the children, why not try to stop the supply of children to orphanages in the first place? What political policies have placed those children in the orphanages? What can be done to support families and allow parents to raise their own children? There are people, thankfully, who express their concern by working in impoverished countries to reunite lost children with family members. Sadly, they are too few and so the punishment continues. Women in economically disadvantaged countries are being punished as we were punished many years ago, by having their children adopted. Our sin was conception outside of marriage. Their sin is poverty. Women in affluent countries must stop punishing other women for being poor and powerless by taking their children from them.

We may sometimes find customs and practices in other countries distressing and difficult to understand and we can say so, but we must allow them to legislate according to their own consciences. We should not simply rush in to "rescue" them from their cultural heritage just because their beliefs are different from ours. For those who are concerned about suffering in other countries, instead of "buying" a child for $25,000.00 and then spending many more thousands of dollars raising that child, they could consider sending their money to an aid agency such as Community Aid Abroad or Oxfam, to help that country feed its children and support them in their families. For countries that are going through difficult times, such as war and acts of aggression, robbing them of their children causes further heartache. In countries where the political climate does not put the needs of families first, it appears that those who connive with them to dispose of their "problem" ie their children are supporting those regimes.

There are many, of course, who prefer not to address these issues. Unfortunately there is a widespread ethnocentrism in so-called "civilised" countries which causes people to assume that living in an English-speaking, affluent country is inherently better than living in a so-called "third world" country. This shows no respect for the intrinsic value of other cultures and their traditions. Some adoptive parents, no doubt, are relieved to think that because they have adopted children from overseas, their adopted children's original families will never be able to find them and that, even if they do, their children will not speak the same language as their family members, nor understand the same culture and so it is unlikely that a close relationship will develop. Some parents of children adopted from other countries, do, of course, take their adopted children back to visit their homeland. This could be because they respect and value the culture of the country in which the child was born. Anecdotal evidence, however, suggests a more sinister motive. Some adoptive parents are disappointed that their adopted children are not sufficiently grateful for having been "rescued" from a miserable existence in their country of origin by being wrenched from their community. Sadly, they take the children there to show them the poverty and squalor from which they have escaped in order to attempt to instil some gratitude in them.

As early as 1977, concerns were being expressed here in Australia about intercountry adoption. At a seminar on intercountry adoption at the University of Adelaide in July, 1977, Marie Mune spoke about, '... some of the global issues involved, particularly ... the relationship between industrial, western and non-industrial eastern countries - and the things that the whole issue of adoption has to say about our attitudes to family, to the ownership of children and something of our attitude to race' (Mune, 1977, p31). Mune pointed out that there were certainly

197

abuses involved. She cited the example of orphanages in Korea, which were run by Christian organisations. Any child who became a resident of those orphanages was automatically designated a Christian child. The orphanage policy was to place children with parents that shared their religious orientation. Of course, it was very difficult to find Christian couples in Korea and so these children were mostly adopted by couples from other countries.

Mune also affirmed that, '... the idea of adoption is very much a western idea' and that, 'Adoption is virtually unknown in Moslem countries' and 'In Africa, again, adoption is practically unknown' (Mune, 1977, p32). Mune, whose partner is Asian, also discussed racism. She said, 'I have the feeling that sometimes, when I'm talking to families, an Asian child is beautiful but an adult Asian isn't so good ... Now this really frightens me' (ibid p32). Mune also mentioned adoptive parents who claim that their adopted children have 'no problems'. Mune says that research on intercountry adoption situations shows that, '... when the parents say the child has no racial problems, the child shows far more social problems. This is just about the only correlation that stands good over several studies. In some way, the parent who says there isn't a problem either is not hearing the child or is refusing to let the child speak' (ibid p32-33). Still on the topic of racism, Mune said, 'The other thing which worries me in attitudes to race is the belief that some people have that by adopting children they are improving race relations in the world' (ibid p33). Mune described the attitude of these adoptive parents as being one of, "We'll ignore what you look like so long as you are like us in every other way and we can bring you up as a child." Mune was also concerned about the adoptive parent, '... who wears the child like a banner, as a sign of their beliefs or their ideals' (ibid p33). Mune added that, 'The person who carried banners about race generally had children who were in trouble and it was fairly clear that the child was being used as a symbol rather than as a real person' (ibid p33). Mune discussed the need for controls. She said, '... we have to recognise that both among the countries which are taking children - through allowing people who may in fact abuse children - and in the countries which are giving children - by the various kinds of abuses that can be involved in getting the children for adoption - there are problems and controls are needed' (ibid p33). Mune spoke of the children from other countries who are being adopted in Australia. She spoke of the, '... continuing search for ways in which we can ensure that the children who come here are not coming because we have set up *a situation which limits the alternatives of parents because we want children'* (ibid p34, italics added).

At the Adoption and Healing conference in New Zealand in 1997, Dr Joyce Maguire Pavao told the story of a Korean boy, adopted into America. The boy's name was Kenny and he was eight years old. He had completed a project on Korea at school. He came home and said to his adoptive mother, "Do you know how many people there are in the whole country of Korea?" He went on to tell his adoptive mother how many millions there were. He then said sadly, "I understand how you told me that my birth mother could not take care of me, but what was wrong with all of those other billions of people?" Pavao commented, 'Kenny was trying to figure out why he was so unlovable that not a single person in a whole country would keep him.' (Pavao, 1997, p199).

The high numbers of intercountry adoptions are testimony to the fact that adoption is still about transferring children from the weak to the powerful, from the poor to the financially secure, only now it is weak countries which are losing their children to powerful countries, poor countries which are losing their children to financially secure countries. This exploitation is insupportable and must stop. Sadly, some people arrogantly assume that children in poor countries mean less to their parents than children in rich countries. The South Australian government has been funding this trade in children for several years and, sadly, there is no sign of this funding coming to an end. As a taxpayer I have expressed my outrage to the government that my taxes are supporting the exploitation of women in poor countries.

The increase in surrogacy arrangements is also a matter for serious concern. Those who support surrogacy obviously have no idea of the bond that grows between mother and child during pregnancy and are not interested in the damage that can be caused by the breaking of that mother-child continuum. If governments familiarised themselves with adoption outcomes, they would not even consider legalising surrogacy arrangements. It appears that some women do not wish to interrupt their careers in order to experience a pregnancy and so choose instead to adopt. Money often changes hands in these arrangements, where it seems that convenience is more important than the mother-child bond.

Surrogacy cases are often misrepresented in the media, especially when the arrangement does not result in the separation of child and mother. The woman who has conceived and carried the child is the mother of the child, not the surrogate mother. A surrogate is someone who replaces the original. The prospective adoptive mother is, in fact, the prospective surrogate mother. The use of the term "surrogate mother" to describe the mother of the child devalues her position as the child's mother and makes it easier to distance her from her child, mentally and emotionally. It is impossible for a woman to make an informed decision to agree to give up her child while she is pregnant. At that stage, she has no way of knowing how she is going to feel when the child is born. The use of the term "biological mother" is offensive to many people, as it suggests a complete lack of emotional bond between mother and child and could only be appropriate where one woman has donated an egg to create a child but has not carried the child. If the mother is a "biological mother" does this make the child a "biological child"? I have said to people in the past that I object to being called my son's "biological mother" as it suggests that my son was conceived in a laboratory; in fact he was conceived in a park.

New technologies in the area of assisting conception have resulted in children being born from anonymously donated sperm and eggs. Children who were created in this way are now adults and are coming forward and complaining that they have been created without any thought for their future desire for information about their ancestry and heritage. They are now having to fight the battles which adopted people have been fighting for many years, to try to obtain access to information which they feel is vital to their sense of identity and their emotional well-being. How sad that consideration was not given to all of the information available about the issues of adopted people, before these children were so thoughtlessly and selfishly created. It seems that financial considerations have taken precedence over human rights issues. Assisted conception is now big business. Anecdotal evidence from infertility counsellors (Speirs, 1998) also suggests that many men who donated sperm in the past are now coming forward to say that they regret that they were not given any advice or counselling at the time about the long term implications of their actions. Some of these men are now providing personal information to clinics to be released if requested by the children.

For each adoption that takes place, many people are affected. Each adopted person has four parents, they may have siblings in their adoptive family and siblings in their natural family (say two of each), they may have a partner themselves and children of their own, perhaps two. This makes an average of twelve people directly affected by each adoption, before we even consider grandparents and other extended family members. In the United States it has been estimated that there are currently six million adopted people. World-wide, there is a vast number of people whose lives have been directly affected by adoption. These are the casualties of adoption. At the International Conference on Adoption and Healing held in New Zealand in 1997, Keith Griffith said, 'Healing needs to be more than running an ambulance at the bottom of the cliff. It must also demand the removal of factors that push people over the top.' (*Adoption and Healing*, 1997, p48).

Perhaps now we can all recognise that those whose lives have been affected by adoption have been damaged by the experience and are entitled to assistance and support. It is time for society to acknowledge that the grief of those who have been separated by adoption is legitimate and is, in fact, the appropriate, expected response to their experiences. Hopefully the community in general will now realise that family members who have been separated by adoption are still family members and that it is natural and commendable for them to wish to know each other.

Let us hope that we can look forward to a more enlightened future, where parents are supported to raise their own children and where everyone recognises that it is wrong to take another person's child, no matter what the circumstances.

∧∧

Bibliography

Anderson, Carole, *Thoughts to Consider for Newly Searching Adoptees*, booklet published by Concerned United Birthparents (CUB) Inc, Des Moines, Iowa, USA, 1997

Bellamy, Louise, *The Painful Legacy of Adoption*, The Age, Melbourne, 1993

Berryman, Sarah, *Understanding Reunion: Reflections on Research from the Post-Adoption Resource Centre, NSW,* in Separation, Reunion, Reconciliation, Proceedings from the Sixth Australian Conference on Adoption, Brisbane, 1997

Bouchier, Patricia, Lambert, Lydia & Triseliotis, John, *Parting with a child for adoption, the mother's perspective,* BAAF, 1991

Condon, John, *Psychological disability in women who relinquish a baby for adoption*, Medical Journal of Australia, Vol.144, Feb 3, 1986.

Dessaix, Robert, *A Mother's Disgrace*, HarperCollins, Sydney, 1994

Doka, Kenneth, *Disenfranchised Grief: Recognizing Hidden Sorrow*, Lexington Books, Lexington, MA., 1989

Doka, Kenneth, *personal correspondence*, 1998

Griffith, Keith, *The legal and social history of adoption in New Zealand*, in Adoption and Healing, Proceedings of the international conference on Adoption and Healing, New Zealand Adoption Education and Healing Trust, 1997

Howe, D., Sawbridge, P. & Hinings, D., *Half a Million Women - Mothers who lose their children by adoption*, Penguin, UK, 1992

Inglis, Kate, *The Relinquishment Process and Grieving*, Third Australian Conference on Adoption, Adelaide, 1982.

Inglis, K., *Living Mistakes - Mothers who consented to adoption*, Allen & Unwin, Sydney, 1984

Kauffman, Jeffrey, *Intrapsychic Dimensions of Disenfranchised Grief*, Chapter 3 in Disenfranchised Grief, edited by Kenneth Doka, Lexington Books, Lexington, MA., 1989

Kuhn, Dale, *A Pastoral Counselor Looks at Silence as a Factor in Disenfranchised Grief*, Chapter 21 in Disenfranchised Grief, edited by Kenneth Doka, Lexington Books, Lexington, MA., 1989

Leitch, David, *Family Secrets*, William Heinemann Ltd, 1984

Lifton, Betty Jean, *Journey of the Adopted Self*, Basic Books, 1994.

Ludbrook, Robert, *Closing the wound*, in Adoption and Healing, Proceedings of the international conference on Adoption and Healing, New Zealand Adoption Education and Healing Trust, 1997

Meagher, David, *The Counselor and the Disenfranchised Griever*, Chapter 27 in Disenfranchised Grief, edited by Kenneth Doka, Lexington Books, Lexington, MA., 1989

Mune, Marie, *Social Welfare Aspects of Intercountry Adoption*, Seminar Proceedings, Department of Adult Education, University of Adelaide, July, 1977.

National BIOETHICS Consultative Committee; *Issues Paper on Infertility Counselling*, prepared by the NBCC Working Group on Counselling for Community Consultation, July, 1990.

Nichols, Jane, *Perinatal Loss*, Chapter 11 in Disenfranchised Grief, edited by Kenneth Doka, Lexington Books, Lexington, MA, 1989.

Pavao, Dr Joyce Maguire, *Healing Stories*, in Adoption and Healing, Proceedings of the international conference on Adoption and Healing, New Zealand Adoption Education and Healing Trust, 1997

Pine, Vanderlyn, *Death, Loss, and Disenfranchised Grief*, Chapter 2 in Disenfranchised Grief, edited by Kenneth Doka, Lexington Books, Lexington, MA., 1989

Proceedings of Third Australian Conference on Adoption, Adelaide, Department of Continuing Education, University of Adelaide, May, 1982

Shannon, Pat, *An Adoptive Parent Retrospective*, Adoption: Past, Present & Future, Conference Proceedings, Auckland, 1994

Shawyer, Joss, *Death by Adoption*, Cicada Press, New Zealand, 1979

Shawyer, Joss, *The Politics of Adoption*, Healthright, Vol.5, No.1, November 1985.

Silverman, Phyllis, *Helping Women Cope with Grief*, Sage Publications, California, 1981

Small, Joanne, *Working with Adoptive Families*, Public Welfare, Summer 1987

Speirs, J. M., *personal correspondence*, 1998

van Keppel, M., Midford, S. & Cicchini, M, *The Experience of Loss in Adoption*, Fifth National Conference, National Association for Loss and Grief, Perth, September, 1987.

Verrier, Nancy, *The Primal Wound: Legacy of Adoption*, presented at the American Congress International Convention, California, USA, April, 1991

Verrier, Nancy, *The Primal Wound*, Gateway Press, Baltimore, USA, 1993

Verrier, Nancy, *Separation Trauma*, in Separation, Reunion, Reconciliation, Proceedings from the Sixth Australian Conference on Adoption, Brisbane, 1997

Winkler, R. & van Keppel, M., *The Effect on the Mother of Relinquishing a Child for Adoption*, Third Australian Conference on Adoption, Adelaide, 1982.

Winkler, R., van Keppel, M., *Relinquishing Mothers in Adoption, Their long-term adjustment,* Melbourne Institute of Family Studies, Monograph no.3, 1984

Worden J. W., *Grief Counselling & Grief Therapy*, Tavistock/Routledge, London, 1982

Stephen's message

This book has been written with the full co-operation and support of my eldest son, Stephen, whom I lost through adoption. This is his statement.

Adoption is not an exact science. When the complexities of people's adoption stories are revealed and you realise how entangled your emotions can be, you are beginning to understand the difficulties faced by everybody touched by adoption. I have found myself condemning its barbarity yet celebrating its uniqueness, for were I not adopted as a baby, I would not be putting pen to paper right now.

Being adopted has given me the benefits of love from two sets of parents and two lots of family members, where the non-adopted have only one - in my opinion you can't have too many people who love you. I also now have two lives running parallel to each other with parts of them never destined to meet although the parts are in some way forever entwined.

My story is the happy face of adoption. I have been lucky enough to have grown up without the hatred, the resentment, the "why me?" syndrome, the rejection and the unfair social stigma. My story has also been a special journey of self-discovery, which has added new and exciting dimensions to my personality along the way.

I am more self-aware - I feel that I know myself better and more positively now that my genetic gaps have been filled in. Every adopted person should search for their natural parents in my opinion: how can you ever expect to truly know yourself if you never know your natural parents?

Shout it loud and be proud.....I was adopted.

Stephen Ferguson, June 1999

Transcript of paper presented at
The Sixth Australian Adoption Conference,
Brisbane, June, 1997.

Grief Associated with the Loss of Children to Adoption

I feel qualified to speak to you on this topic for three reasons. Firstly, I am the natural mother of an adopted son; I gave up my son for adoption in 1970. Secondly, I have been a member of ARMS for 8 years and in that time I have listened to and read about many other natural mothers. Thirdly, I am a social worker and as part of my social work degree, I chose the topic Bereavement and Loss and I made an academic study of the grief associated with the loss of children to adoption. What I have to say to you today is based on my own experience, the experiences of many other relinquishing mothers and the academic research on the topic, such as it is. I'd like to explain to you the path that I took to reach the conclusion I have reached.

Most of you are probably familiar with Dr Condon's study of relinquishing mothers in South Australia and of Winkler and van Keppel's study of relinquishing mothers Australia wide. They found that not only did women not recover emotionally from giving up a child to adoption, but that their anger and sense of loss actually increased over time. I found that very interesting because it seemed to contradict community expectations of the process of grief. When we suffer other types of losses in our lives, the sadness generally decreases as time goes by, which is why people talk about time being such a great healer. For some reason time was not healing relinquishing mothers.

Why should this type of grief situation be the exact opposite of what one might expect? I set out to find the answer to this question. I searched my own experience, the experiences of the women I had encountered and the literature on the subject. Well, I say the literature on the subject, but, of course, there is very little literature on this particular subject. And so I had to begin at the beginning and work my way through what was available. I started with a study of grief. I read books on grief and grief counselling. It became obvious to me that the models of grief counselling I was reading about wouldn't work with relinquishing mothers. But why wouldn't they work? I realised that the grief of relinquishment was fundamentally different from other types of grief.

But it must have something in common with some types of grief, surely? I explored grief associated with abortion, with stillbirth and neo-natal death, with loss of custody. Yes, there were some similarities, but relinquishment grief was unique. Someone asked me to consider the possibility that relinquishment grief was a form of disenfranchised grief. Perhaps this would help me to understand relinquishment grief better.

I read a book called "Disenfranchised Grief" by Kenneth Doka. It was very interesting and the notion of disenfranchised grief appealed to me, but nowhere in his book did he mention relinquishment. He talked about the grief you experience when you lose your budgie, the grief you experience when your secret homosexual lover leaves you, but he didn't address the grief of relinquishing mothers.

Anyway, I decided to apply Doka's definition of disenfranchised grief and see if it fitted with what I already knew about relinquishment grief. Doka says grief is disenfranchised when the grief is connected with a loss which cannot be openly acknowledged, publicly mourned or socially supported. He also says that in many cases of disenfranchised grief, the relationship is not recognised, the loss is not recognised or the griever is not recognised. Everything fitted. Giving up a child for adoption becomes a loss which cannot be openly acknowledged, which is why relinquishing mothers often suffer in silence. Giving up a child for adoption is never publicly mourned because relinquishing mothers are so busy pretending it never happened. And it certainly isn't socially supported. Any attempt we made to convey our grief to someone after the event was met with either, 'Well it was your choice so you can't complain', or 'You did the right thing, what are you so upset about?', or 'Well it's done now, no use crying over spilt milk'.

Doka says that people who have experienced a loss often feel anger, guilt, sadness, depression, hopelessness and numbness and that in cases of disenfranchised grief, these feelings can persist for a very long time. Doka states that mourners whose grief is disenfranchised are by virtue of this cut off from social supports and so have few opportunities to express and resolve their grief and that the result can be that they feel alienated from their community. Doka also says that the lack of recognition of their grief often results in them holding on to it more tenaciously than they might otherwise have done. Yes, everything fitted. I actually wrote to Kenneth Doka to point out to him that he'd forgotten to include the chapter on relinquishment, but he didn't reply.*

Then I studied various models of grief counselling. I chose Worden's book, "Grief Counselling and Grief Therapy" as a fairly representative example. Worden says that mourning is necessary in order to re-establish equilibrium. The necessary components of grief work, according to Worden, are a series of tasks. The first is to accept the reality of the loss, the second is to experience the pain of grief, the third to adjust to the environment from which the lost person is missing and the fourth to withdraw emotional energy and reinvest it in another relationship. Personally I think that last task is very suspect anyway, in any grief situation. According to Worden, grief becomes repressed or delayed when there are no opportunities to perform these tasks.

It is my opinion that it is because relinquishment grief is disenfranchised, that relinquishing mothers are unable to perform the grief work which would assist them towards resolution of their grief. They are often unable to perform Worden's first task, to accept the reality of their loss, because they have no concrete focus for their grief. Many of them never saw their child, never held their child, never named their child; they received no birth certificate to prove that their child had really been born. In cases of stillbirth and neo-natal death bonding is now actively encouraged, in order to facilitate the grieving process. In most relinquishment cases, however, bonding was deliberately prevented. For relinquishing mothers there is also no finality to their loss. As far as they are aware, their child is still alive. Their loss is shrouded in uncertainty. Is my child alive or dead, will I ever see my child again? Will this pain ever be over? Condon points out the similarity between women who have given up children for adoption and relatives of those missing in action during war time. He states that in both cases the lack of finality causes disabling chronic grief reactions.

Relinquishing mothers are unable to perform Worden's second task, to experience the pain of grief, because they have no opportunities to express their grief. In many cases the pregnancy and birth took place in secret and was hidden from most people. After the event, the mothers were told to put it behind them and not to dwell on it. I have yet to meet a relinquishing mother who was offered counselling after her child was born. Relinquishing mothers were not permitted to grieve. Their sadness made others feel uncomfortable. Worden says that when the pain of grief is avoided or suppressed then depression often follows. Depression is common in relinquishing mothers and it sometimes continues for many years. It is often the result of the fact that relinquishing mothers hid their pain. Apparent absence of grief can actually be a sign of acute grief which has been repressed or delayed. Those relinquishing mothers who are finally given permission to mourn often are surprised at the depth of their pain, even many years after their loss.

Relinquishing mothers are unable to perform Worden's third task, to adjust to the environment from which the lost person is missing, because society never accorded their child a position in the mother's life. And the environment itself has changed irrevocably. Many relinquishing mothers had to leave their employment when they became pregnant and move to a new area. For many of them it was the end of their relationship with the child's father. The pregnancy also caused an irreversible change in the relationship between a relinquishing mother and her parents. And so the birth of the child was often coupled with other stressful life events. Having had a child made them feel different from their friends, whom they often resented for being so carefree and hopeful for the future. Relinquishing mothers felt that they had changed fundamentally and they couldn't go back to the place they had previously held in society. Expecting a woman who has carried a child for nine months, given birth and then had her motherhood denied, to carry on as if nothing has happened is just quite unrealistic.

It is impossible for relinquishing mothers to perform Worden's fourth task, to withdraw emotional energy from the relationship and reinvest it in another relationship because the relationship has not ended. The child still exists. Many women, almost half of those who relinquish, are unable to have any further children. They are unable to invest any emotion in another relationship. In some cases their physical body refuses to co-operate and in other cases they feel a sense of loyalty to their lost child which prevents them from producing what may be seen by some as a replacement child.

Everything I read about grief resolution from then on was informed by my conviction that the grief of relinquishment was disenfranchised. I read about the role of ritual in grief resolution and the purposes of funeral rites. These include; announcing the death, recognising the place which the dead person held in society, assisting the bereaved through the process of grief, delimiting the period of mourning, allowing the grievers to express their emotions publicly and allowing the members of the community to gather to support each other. Rituals provide the bereaved with permission to mourn.

There is no ritual surrounding a relinquishment. There is no public announcement of either the birth or the relinquishment; far from it. In many cases the intention was to keep that information from as many people as possible. There is no recognition of the place which the child held in the society, because the child who was born becomes a non-existent person after adoption. Once the new birth certificate is issued, that original child has no place in society because society denies the child's existence. No one assists the relinquishing mother through the process of grief. To be honest, I think no one knew how to. Relinquishing mothers

v

were not allowed to express their emotions publicly. They had to hide their feelings after the birth the way they had learned to hide them throughout their pregnancies. And in the case of relinquishment the community does not gather round the person who is grieving; in fact they often avoid her. There is no public outpouring of grief. There are no photographs, no mementoes. For relinquishing mothers there are no rituals to provide limits to the period of mourning. That's why we feel as if it will never end.

I read about intrapsychic disenfranchisement. This occurs when the mourner feels responsible for the loss and it results in feelings of shame and guilt. Like many women, when I found out I was pregnant for the first time, I suddenly found myself in a situation for which I was totally unprepared and I reacted in the only way I knew how. But, because of our experience, we relinquishing mothers often disenfranchise ourselves. We believe that we don't fit, that we're not as good as other women. We feel that we are not entitled to grieve and so we suppress our own grief. As a result we cut ourselves off from some possible sources of support.

I read about the role of silence in grief suppression. In many cases of relinquishment, the pregnancy was hidden and so silence was inevitable. In other cases, people knew about the baby, but it seemed as if the whole of society was part of a conspiracy of silence, with everyone pretending it hadn't happened. The fact that our children were issued with a second birth certificate which denied our existence only added to the communal denial of our experience. Winkler and van Keppel state that, ' the current practices of altering birth certificates and maintaining closed records ... perpetuate the unresolvable grief experienced by ... relinquishing mothers'. Why did we join this conspiracy of silence? Because we interpreted this community silence as disapproval. We didn't feel that it would be safe to express our grief. We felt betrayed; betrayed by a society which told us to be unselfish and give our children away for their own good and then made us feel ashamed of it afterwards.

Relinquishing mothers were never given permission to mourn. It's no wonder then that many of us feel that we have never quite regained our equilibrium. I believe that all of this explains why

vi

relinquishing mothers report that their sadness and anger have increased with time. Taking into account everything which I have discovered about grief, that is to be expected. I think it's important to say that and so I'll say it again. It is to be expected that relinquishing mothers have not resolved their grief. They have been denied every opportunity to perform grief work because their grief has been disenfranchised in the ways I have described.

What are the outcomes of this for relinquishing mothers? They experience the same outcomes as other people whose grief is disenfranchised and unresolved. They become depressed, they have low self-esteem, they develop emotional disturbances and psychosomatic illnesses. They withdraw from society, they succumb to substance abuse, they have difficulty forming healthy relationships. Their mourning becomes chronic. They often have difficulty dealing with subsequent losses, because, according to Doka, "...the old disenfranchisement will affect the new situation and may enforce a repetition of the earlier inhibited grief pattern". This means that because we did not learn how to grieve productively in what for most of us was the first major loss in our lives, we simply don't know how to do it and so when we experience other losses in our lives we tend to repeat the pattern of behaviour that applied at the time of our relinquishment and suppress our grief again.

If any or all of this applies to you, then it's not because you have always been emotionally unstable. It's because you have suffered a grievous loss in your life which has not been acknowledged. Doka states that the central issue in dealing with disenfranchised grief is to validate the loss. That is the first step towards grief resolution. On the topic of grief resolution, I'd like to read a quotation from Kate Inglis's book, 'Living Mistakes', which expresses very poignantly the predicament of the relinquishing mother:

Which particular thing is she to accept...that she has a child who is lost to her but not dead; that she was responsible for its loss on the day she surrendered the legal rights and obligations of parenthood; that she lives in a world in which some mothers are rewarded and others punished for their fertility; that most people failed her, that she failed herself; that she did the right thing; that she did the wrong thing; that she grieves, that grief is not appropriate; that she is unnatural in her ability to take such a course; that she is natural in thinking of her baby before herself or conversely of thinking of herself before the baby; that she was, and still is, isolated in her experience; that her grief cannot be resolved and must somehow be lived with alone? What is she to accept to reach the tranquillity glowingly described as following acceptance in the most commonly used grief theory model. Must she also now accept another failure; ie to successfully deal with her grief?

We should not feel that we have failed because there are very good reasons why we have not resolved our grief. For those same reasons we may never resolve it. Phyllis Silverman wrote a book called "Helping Women Cope with Grief". In it she says of the relinquishing mother, "...instead of blaming society for denying her the right to mourn openly, she begins to blame herself for not being able to behave the way those around her would prefer". We should not feel guilty or inadequate because we have not resolved our grief, because we still shed tears for our lost children. We, as relinquishing mothers, are tired of being pressured to meet other people's expectations. We want our loss to be validated and our grief to be acknowledged. We don't want to be held responsible if our grief has become pathological. We don't want our grief to be invalidated by being told that we "did the right thing".

I'd like to refer again to Kate Inglis's book, "Living Mistakes". In it she talks about the anger experienced by many relinquishing mothers. She says, "...she may begin her pregnancy in anger and resentment and continue for years with a randomly placed rage". I identified with that immediately. I not only began my pregnancy in anger and resentment, I spent my whole pregnancy in anger and resentment. I have carried my anger inside me for 28 years, like Tam O'Shanter's wife, 'nursing her wrath to keep it warm'. My rage is constantly fuelled by the many tragic stories I have heard of the sufferings of family members separated by adoption. I like to think now that my rage is not 'randomly placed'. I know exactly what it is I am angry about and I like to think that I use my rage productively now. I believe it is my 'rage' which led me to investigate the grief experienced by relinquishing mothers. I am angry at the suggestions that we are somehow inherently defective because we cannot resolve our grief. I resent the fact that I am still being told to get over it and get on with it and don't dwell on it.

Why do I feel it is necessary to say all of this? If you're a relinquishing mother, I'm saying it to you so that you'll understand why you can't make peace with yourself over your relinquishment. If you're an adopted person, I'm saying it to you so that you can begin to appreciate some of the difficulties which your natural mother has had to face. If you're a member of the helping professions who may come in contact with relinquishing mothers, I'm saying it to you so that you can begin to understand the depth of their pain. If you are a person who is in a position to influence government policy then what I am saying to you is, "Don't let this happen to any more women. Put a stop to it". And I'm saying it to the world in general because people are so ignorant of our experiences and our issues. I am angry now at what I and many women have suffered but more so at the fact that women are still suffering in Australia and in other countries because they are being separated from their children by adoption.

Nothing can change what happened to us in the past, but it is wrong for women now to be allowed to suffer the same agonies that we have suffered. And it is wrong of society to permit it. My rage has driven me to educate myself and now it drives me on to try to educate other people about the effects of relinquishment. My rage drives me to talk about relinquishment issues to anyone who will listen and to write copious letters to newspaper editors and to politicians.

And what conclusion did I reach in the end? Did I decide that relinquishment grief cannot be resolved? Not necessarily, no. The conclusion I reached is that it is not surprising that we have not been able to resolve our grief because our grief is complicated and deep. The conclusion I reached is that we must accept that our grief is complicated and not feel inadequate if we are still suffering, but that we should be working all the time towards an understanding of our grief and a resolution of our grief, bearing in mind that total resolution may well be an unrealistic goal.

*At the time of presenting the paper, Dr Doka had not yet responded to my letter, but he did at a later date. (Author)

Transcript of paper presented at
British Association of Social Workers Seminar
Edinburgh, 13 August 1998

*Disenfranchised grief: recognising and meeting the needs of birth
parents who have lost children to adoption*

I bring to this subject not just my social work experience but also
my personal experience; not just my professional knowledge but
also my personal passion. I make no apology for my emotional
response to adoption issues. I believe that it does not compete
with my professional commitment, but rather strengthens it. I am
the natural mother of an adult, adopted child. I am also a social
worker. My child was born and adopted here in Scotland and so I
have experienced firsthand the Scottish adoption system. I have
lived in Australia for the last sixteen years and so I have
experienced there the availability of post-adoption services. As my
son and I traced each other with the assistance of Scottish
agencies, however, I have also had experience of some of the
post-adoption services available in Scotland. I should like to begin
by outlining why I feel natural parents are entitled to post-adoption
services and then go on to explore how I believe those services
can be provided in the most helpful ways. I refer mostly to natural
mothers because the work I have done has mostly been with
women. I acknowledge, however, that natural fathers also grieve
the loss of their children and are just as entitled to an appropriate
service to assist them.

For many years, members of the helping professions and
members of the community in general have chosen to believe that
women who have given up children for adoption have acted in the
best interests of their children, have parted with their children
voluntarily and so have not suffered greatly as a result of their
loss. In fact, nothing could be further from the truth. This belief,
however, allows society and the social work profession to feel

more comfortable with the system of adoption, which has been operating for many years to transfer children from the weak to the powerful.

When my son was born, here in Edinburgh in 1970, there was, as far as I can recall, no understanding that women, like me, who had lost children to adoption, would benefit from post-adoption support. I am quite sure that I was never offered any such assistance. My relationship with the hospital almoner was not a happy one. I was a very reluctant client and I did not ever view her as a support person. In fact, I so resented what I regarded as her intrusiveness that, given the opportunity, I simply lied to her. With hindsight it seems to us remarkably naive and ignorant of society to have expected women like me to simply put the loss of our children behind us and carry on as if it had never happened. We did not, of course and there are very good reasons why we did not. Research has shown that the effects of losing a child to adoption are both negative and long-lasting.

A great deal has been written by social workers and academics about grief work and grief resolution. I lost my first born child and that loss was the first major loss in my life. It was complicated by other related losses. Unfortunately, I was unable at the time to mourn those losses. The people who told me to put it behind me and get on with my life were actually denying my loss and encouraging me to suppress my grief. And, of course, that is exactly what I, and thousands of other women, did. We suppressed our grief and suffered the consequences.

At times of bereavement, there are certain rituals and behaviours which are acceptable and expected in our society. If you have lost a loved one, you will most likely receive cards, flowers, telephone calls and visits. Sympathy will be expressed. Assistance will be offered. There will be discussion about the lost family member, questions about their passing, reminiscences about their life. There will be a gathering of family and friends to farewell the person who has died and to comfort the bereaved. All of these rituals and behaviours assist the bereaved to come to terms with their loss and to face the future, knowing they are not alone.

When my first son was born, I did not receive any cards nor flowers. There was no announcement of his birth in the newspaper. There were no gifts for him. My hospital ward contained forty mothers and thirty-nine babies. My mother tried to visit my son in the hospital nursery and was turned away by the nurse. His birth was a very lonely event, for him and for me. I know my experience was similar to that of many other women who lost children to adoption.

There was no gathering of the community around us when we lost our children. In fact, our family and friends often turned their backs on us because our situation embarrassed them and made them feel uncomfortable. There was no encouragement for us to share our feelings. In fact, our feelings were denied because we were told we were "doing the right thing". There were no rituals to help us to accept our loss and in most cases our children were simply never referred to again. Many women were not allowed to see or hold their children and so they had no concrete focus for their grief. Those of us who did see our children knew what we had lost at the time of relinquishing them, but it was impossible for us to comprehend what we had lost in terms of the future. Our loss had no finality, as we knew our children would go on living somewhere without us. Because we were ashamed of what had happened and we were afraid of other people's reactions, we joined the conspiracy of silence. We denied our children, pretended they had never been born and by doing so, we denied our grief also.

Our grief was disenfranchised. Disenfranchised grief is grief which is not openly acknowledged, socially supported nor publicly mourned. The grief of natural mothers was usually not openly acknowledged. Many pregnancies and births took place in secret and even when there was no secrecy surrounding the birth, the mother did not usually share her grief with anyone. Instead she shed secret tears. Our grief was not socially supported as we had placed ourselves in a position which was unacceptable to society. Society's response to our position was to encourage us to reverse it; to change from being mothers to being ex-mothers by allowing other women to mother our children. Our grief was not publicly mourned because we were an embarrassment. We were to blame. We were made to feel ashamed and the general feeling was that we had no right to mourn.

In cases of bereavement, where grief is socially supported, the feelings of loss gradually resolve over time. When grief is disenfranchised, however, this does not happen. When grief is denied and suppressed, in fact, rather than diminishing, it actually grows. It grows silently and painfully. Research conducted in Australia shows that women who have lost children to adoption reported that their feeling of anger and their sense of loss actually increased with the passage of time. It is no wonder that these women also reported a higher incidence of depression and anxiety than the general population.

Unfortunately, because of the lack of understanding in the general community and among professionals, women who have lost children to adoption have been reluctant to seek help. They have often spent many years, alone with their grief, silently apologising. They apologised for becoming pregnant when they were unmarried, they apologised for giving away their children, they later apologised for not having resolved their grief and not being "successful" at putting their loss behind them. My goal is to convince these women and others in the community, that there is no need for them to apologise. Their long term grief is the natural reaction to the huge loss which they suffered and to the fact that their grief could not be resolved because it was unrecognised and therefore unsupported by society. Their loss has been invalidated by family and friends and also by professionals. Because natural mothers have been systematically denied all of the components of supposedly successful grief work, their grief has become chronic and has remained unresolved.

The grief of natural mothers is caused by adoption policy and practice and it can never be resolved until it is acknowledged and validated. Governments *created* adoption policy and practice and governments have a responsibility to provide a service that will assist natural mothers to address their grief issues. Social workers *enacted* adoption policy and practice and I believe that they also have a responsibility to support the needs of natural parents for appropriate post-adoption services. I was heartened to read in the

Regulations and Guidance for The Children (Scotland) Act 1995 that there is a recognition that the natural parents of adopted children are entitled to a service in their own right. I was very disheartened, however, to read also in those regulations, that, "Agencies are required to offer counselling to birth parents if they have a problem about adoption". I find it difficult to express the extent of my dismay and anger at such a statement. It seems to me to display a profound and, for me, very distressing lack of understanding of the issues for natural parents. I am personally very insulted by this implication. *If women who have lost children to adoption do not resolve their grief, this does not illustrate some deficiency on their part.*

I am saddened and angered by the fact that there is no legal right in Scotland for natural mothers to access information regarding their adult, adopted children. In my view it is ironic that Scotland boasts of an 'open' adoption system. It may be open to adopted people. It remains quite closed to natural mothers. As far as I am aware, there is no co-ordinated post-adoption service for women in Scotland who have lost children to adoption. Services appear to be provided in an arbitrary fashion by a variety of agencies, most of which seem to be also involved with arranging adoptions. It took my son and me three years to contact each other. His was a private adoption and so there was no adoption agency involved. Taking different advice, we had each approached different agencies for assistance. Because there was no co-operation between the agencies, our efforts were for a long time unsuccessful. Our reunion was, in the end, as much a result of our combined efforts as it was the result of an amazing coincidence and could well never have happened. This situation does not, in my opinion, constitute a satisfactory post-adoption service for natural parents.

Adoption legislation in Australia is a state-based matter, not regulated by federal government. Each state passes its own adoption laws. I am familiar with the adoption legislation in South Australia, where I live and I know that other states have similar legislation and that there are general trends Australia-wide, with, however, state-based idiosyncrasies. In South Australia, adoption legislation changed with the introduction of The Adoption Act (1988). Prior to this major change in adoption legislation, there was a great deal of community consultation. There were public meetings, written and oral submissions to government and a great deal of media coverage. As a result of the changes introduced by this act, adopted people and natural parents now have equal rights to access adoption information. This means that when adopted people are eighteen years of age, they can obtain all of the information held by the appropriate government department regarding the circumstances of their adoption, including the names and addresses of their natural parents. Natural parents of adult, adopted children can also obtain all information held by the department regarding the adoption of their child, including the new name given to their child after adoption and the address at which the adoptive parents were living at the time of the adoption. From this information, it is usually a relatively uncomplicated procedure to trace the party or parties involved. For adoptions which took place prior to 1988, unfortunately, there is the facility for either party to prevent the release of identifying information. For adoptions which have taken place since 1988, however, this facility does not exist. Adoption information is provided to those who apply by the Department of Family and Community Services, which also offers counselling or referrals to relevant agencies.

In South Australia, I am Deputy Chairperson of an organisation called the Australian Relinquishing Mothers Society, known as ARMS, which is a support group for the natural mothers of adopted children. ARMS was founded in South Australia in 1982 and received government funding in 1989, after the new adoption act came into effect. Our current situation is that we receive a government grant which allows us to employ a social worker and a clerical worker on a part-time basis. ARMS is run by a management committee of volunteers. Our organisation is fundamentally a self-help group and decisions and policies are made by natural mothers. We offer one-to-one counselling with the social worker, therapeutic groups with the social worker, support groups run by the members and telephone support provided by members of management committee. ARMS also takes a very active role in raising community awareness of adoption issues. We conduct a phone-in every Mother's Day. We set up displays in shopping centres and we organise media coverage whenever possible. We try to maintain a high profile in the community and are often invited by the media to express our opinions on adoption issues. We feel that we serve natural mothers well by combining the services of a social worker who is totally devoted to their needs with the benefits of a self-help programme.

Natural parents deserve and need a satisfactory and appropriate post-adoption service. I should like to explore the type of service which might best suit their needs.

Although I believe that governments have a responsibility to provide post-adoption services for natural parents, I also believe that those services must *not* be provided by workers who are also helping to arrange adoptions. As the natural mother of an adopted child, I would never consult a social worker, nor an agency, which was involved in adoption placement, for assistance with my adoption issues. This has been described by one woman in Australia as like being asked to attend your rapist for a smear test. Agencies, and the social workers employed by them, who are actively involved in arranging adoptions, are perpetuating the system which caused my grief and pain in the first place. They are currently causing pain for other women like myself by actively supporting the policies and practices which separate them from their children. Post-adoption services for natural mothers must be completely separate from adoption placement services.

For workers in post-adoption services to be helpful to natural mothers, they must have an understanding of the nature of post-relinquishment grief and a commitment to supporting women in addressing their grief issues. If you are working in this area, you should be aware from the outset that post-relinquishment grief is complicated and that by the time women seek help, it has often become chronic. Addressing post-relinquishment grief issues is usually a long, slow process and progress is not always steady. It will not proceed at all unless there is an understanding and acknowledgement on the part of the worker that post-relinquishment grief is unlike other types of grief in fundamental ways.

Post-relinquishment grief has been denied. It has not been recognised nor validated by the community in general nor by professionals. The first step for the worker is to acknowledge the existence and validity of post-relinquishment grief and to assure natural mothers that their grief is the natural response to their loss. Work towards resolution will not proceed without this acceptance on the part of the mother as well as the worker. It is not easy to try to facilitate productive grieving so long after the event, but only when the grief is brought to the surface can it be addressed.

Post-relinquishment grief is further complicated by the issues of shame and blame. Women are not assisted either by being told that they were totally responsible for the decision to have their child adopted, nor by being told that they had no choice in the matter at all. In very few cases is either of these statements accurate. A frank and intense exploration of the circumstances which led to the loss of the child is a very valuable starting point.

If a mother has approached you as a worker for assistance, then she has already broken her silence. She has disclosed her status to you, but there may be others in her life who are still unaware that she has relinquished a child. She will need support to acknowledge her child in the wider community.

The lack of resolution of post-relinquishment grief can lead to poor patterns of grief resolution which can follow a woman through the subsequent losses in her life. An exploration of the history of losses which have occurred and the ways in which those losses have affected the natural mother can also be very valuable. For many women the loss of their child to adoption was the first major loss in their lives and because their grief at that loss was disenfranchised, they have been unable to develop productive grieving techniques.

Post-relinquishment grief is also complicated by the lack of finality. The mother is grieving the loss of a child who probably still exists, but whose childhood is lost to her forever. I encourage natural mothers, without exception, to search for their lost children. If children are removed from their mothers by physical force, we expect mothers to do everything in their power to find them again. Our children were also taken from us by force - not by physical force but by the force of public opinion, which persuaded us that our children would be better off being raised apart from us. Women who have lost children to adoption need to receive acknowledgement that it is perfectly natural for them to want to find their lost children. It is, in fact, a healthy response to their loss. I look forward to the day when this is supported in Scotland by legislation which will actively support mothers in searching for their children. It is important to understand, however, that the process of grief resolution does not cease with reunion. Reunion itself is a traumatic experience and ongoing support and acceptance are vital after mothers have met their lost children again.

The role of support groups cannot be overstated. Natural mothers have felt for many years marginalised and abandoned by society. It is very empowering for them to meet even one other woman who has also lost a child to adoption. The ideal post-adoption service for natural mothers, in my view, would combine professional expertise with a self-help component.

Emphasis in South Australia is currently on the best interests of children. For this reason, programmes which concentrate on family preservation and family reunification receive government support. When a child is considered to be at risk, efforts are made first of all to support the natural family to provide a safe environment for their child. If this is not successful, attempts are made to place the child within the extended family or to find carers within the community with which the child is familiar. Only as a last resort are children placed with total strangers. In very few cases do adoptions take place. Regardless of the nature of the placement, on-going contact with the child's natural family is encouraged and supported.

In the early 1970s in South Australia, there were approximately one thousand adoptions per year. In South Australia last year, there were only six adoptions of Australian-born children. There are no longer any step-parent adoptions nor adoptions by family members and there has never been a tradition of adoptions without consent. Government funding for adoptions of children from other countries has been withdrawn* and I am confident that those adoptions also will shortly cease. I predict that, in the near future, transfer of children from the weak to the powerful, whether it be from young, single women to financially secure, partnered women or from weak, troubled countries to stable, prosperous countries, will no longer be considered to be socially and morally acceptable and will cease. I firmly believe that, in Australia, within a relatively short space of time, adoption will disappear completely.

In the meantime, there is, of course, still an on-going need for an effective post-adoption service. Efforts must continue to be made to repair the emotional damage caused by past adoption policy as adoption has caused an enormous amount of pain and grief to a huge number of people. I hope that a service will develop, in Scotland, along the lines which I have indicated and that natural mothers here will benefit from increased awareness of their issues and increased understanding of their grief, both among society in general, but more particularly among those in the helping professions. I should like to see the social work profession in Scotland convert the private pain of women who have lost children to adoption into a public issue by actively supporting their right to a quality post-adoption service.

*At the time of delivering this seminar paper, the author believed this to be the case. In fact, government funding in South Australia for overseas adoptions had not yet ceased at the time of going to print. (Author)